3
9|12
2

10/22/07

"Tim O'Brien has decisively moved the personal branding discipline forward. His work is groundbreaking, provocative, creative, fun and a must-read for anyone who wants greater influence."

PETER MONTOYA
Author, *The Brand Called You*

"This book is a fabulous educational tool for building a career that matters."

CRAIG ROBBINS
Chief Knowledge Officer
"The Dean" of Colliers University
Colliers International

"There is no doubt about it. This book can take your game to the next level—and beyond. I recommend it to all of my fellow Marines. They will recognize many of the truths we live by. *Semper Fi,* Tim O'Brien!"

STEWART NAVARRE
Colonel, USMC, Chief of Staff for
Marine Corps Installation West

"This book is a must for every athlete who wants to be a champion on the field and in the business community."

ROMAN PHIFER
NFL Linebacker
3-time Superbowl Champion

The POWER of
PERSONAL
BRANDING

The POWER of
PERSONAL
BRANDING

Creating Celebrity Status with Your Target Audience

TIM O'BRIEN

THE PERSONAL BRANDING GROUP, INC.
Los Angeles, California 90071

Author: Timothy P. O'Brien, Esq.

Book design: Lightbourne, Inc.

Cover photographs: GettyImages.com

President Washington, One Dollar Bill, Photodisc Green, Ryan McVay
John, F. Welch Jr., Getty Images News, Porter Gifford
Tiger Woods, Getty Images Sport, Jeff Golden
Princess Diana, Tim Graham Photo Library, Tim Graham
Oprah Winfrey, Getty Images Entertainment, Paul Hawthorne
Tom Hanks, Getty Images Entertainment, In Focus
President Reagan, Time & Life Pictures, Diana Walker

Manufactured in U.S.A.

First Printing, March 2007
First Published, May 2007

10 9 8 7 6 5 4 3 2 1

ISBN 10: 0-9714589-0-1
ISBN 13: 978-0-9714589-0-1

Library of Congress Catalog Number : 2006930947

*To the number one personal brand
in our home—my bride,
Patricia.*

Check out our blogs:
www.thepersontosee.com
and
www.timobriendaily.com

Acknowledgments

Thank you to all my colleagues who took time out of their very busy schedules to give me feedback on some or all of this manuscript, most notably Chris Rising, Seth Gilman, Robert Pagliarini, Phil Glosserman, Robert Brunswick, Eric Snyder, David Fenton, James Kropff, Brian Kabateck, Todd Ackerman, Ray Bayat and Murad Siam. Your feedback was invaluable.

To Grace Kono-Wells at Keystrokes, who went above and beyond the call of duty to meet all of our typing deadlines.

To my sister, Eileen T. Davis and to Suzy Mullen and Elizabeth Klussmann, all of whom worked ably to coordinate the organization and completion of this book.

Preface

When I set out to write this book, I wanted to produce more than just another vanilla "how to" business book. Rather, my objective has always been to provoke thought, challenge my readers to reevaluate the way they present themselves to their marketplaces and, most of all, help all of us understand that, regardless of job title, net worth or age, we all need to be working on our personal brand until the day we die.

At times I have inserted my own opinions about who I believe does and does not have a great personal brand. Additionally, I have been fairly blunt about what my experience has taught me regarding what works and what does not work when it comes to building a great personal brand. Feel free to disagree with my examples and opinions. That's the essence of personal branding; it is not an exact science. It is very much a "beauty is in the eye of the beholder" discipline.

As you work through each chapter, I encourage you to keep your eye on the ball. Take what works for you and implement it. That which doesn't, disregard.

Good luck!

Contents

Introduction

Can you guess the identity of this person?

- Under his leadership, a war was started under false pretenses.
- He never distinguished himself personally in battle and yet was hailed by many, including those in the military, as a great leader.
- He presided over a war that seemed to drag on and on.
- He made poor strategic military decisions that caused the loss of thousands of American lives.
- He stubbornly refused to change his war strategy despite diminishing public support.
- During the war, he appeared to act at times like an American dictator.
- He practiced self-aggrandizing theatrics in connection with the war in order to make himself look good.
- He never held a real job in the business marketplace as an adult. Most of his wealth came from inheritance.

By now, most of you have surely made up your minds about who this person is. If you guessed George, you are correct. But it's not George W. Bush—it's George Washington. Here are the facts:

- In 1753, young George Washington was a Lieutenant Colonel in the British Army. The British controlled an area that was known at that time as the Ohio Country. The French were also making a claim to this land. At one point, the British and French Armies came face-to-face. The French general, in a diplomatic gesture, advanced on foot to inform Washington on the French's position. With Washington looking on, one of his men advanced and struck the French general on the head with a hatchet, instantly killing him. That single blow effectively started the French and Indian War.

- Washington, himself, never did anything particularly heroic in battle. In fact, in the French and Indian War, the regiments under Lieutenant Colonel Washington's command suffered two very humiliating defeats. At Ft. Necessity, Washington's men were all but massacred. During the Battle of Monongahela, Washington's troops suffered 900 casualties. The French and Indian forces just 23. During the Revolutionary War, Washington was equally unimpressive as a combat general. The regiments he led won only two battles. During the war's two biggest battles—Saratoga and Yorktown—Washington was little more than a spectator.

- The Revolutionary War lasted eight long years.

- Eager to avenge the embarrassing loss at Bunker Hill, the British chased Washington's Continental Army to Long Island. Despite the steadfast urgings of his advisors, Washington refused to retreat to avoid an all-out confrontation with the entire British Army and Navy. As a result, the entire 16,000-man Continental Army was crushed to the point of near annihilation.

- During the war, Washington asked for, and received, from the Continental Congress full dictatorial powers.

- The Revolutionary War started in Boston in July 1775, reached its peak between late 1775 and early 1776, but dragged on until 1782. Things got so bad that:
  - States refused to impose taxes to support the war.
  - States also refused to fulfill their militia quotas.

- In the final battle of the Revolutionary War, at Yorktown, Washington was again essentially a spectator. Yet he very publicly hopped into a foxhole next to 21-year-old Thomas Smith, a six-year veteran of the war, and instructed young Smith "to keep it down lest the British sentries hear" him. The reason for Washington's theatrics was so history would remember him as part of the action.
- The evening after the battle of Yorktown, before anyone knew the war was over, Washington prowled around the camp with an axe on his shoulder reportedly "looking for somewhere to get involved."
- Washington's wealth came from inheritance. His wife, Martha, was the richest widow in Virginia when Washington married her.

Despite all of these missteps, Washington is considered, in the words of one of his biographers, Joseph Ellis, to be the "Foundingest" of all the Fathers, even though:

- Franklin was wiser
- Hamilton smarter
- Adams more well-read
- Jefferson more intellectually robust
- Madison more politically astute

A major reason for Washington's exalted status was the effort he put into managing his personal brand. I am not suggesting that Washington does not deserve his place in history as a titanic figure. Ellis makes it abundantly clear that America very well may not be the great country it is today had Washington not been present at its beginning. His nemesis, King George III of England, likewise remarked at the conclusion of the war, "If Washington does indeed refuse the monarchial title and retire as he said he would, Washington would go down as the greatest man in the world." What I am saying is that the persona of George Washington that we know today was very much influenced by the personal brand management of the great man himself.

We know George Washington not necessarily for who he truly was or for what he did and didn't accomplish, but rather mostly the way Washington himself wanted history to remember him. Ellis attributes much of Washington's success to his "courage, composure, and incredible self-control."

The lesson we should learn from Washington's example is that personal brand identity and what our personal brand stands for are oftentimes more influential than our track record. A stellar track record built upon intelligence, skill and hard work is certainly a prerequisite for competing at the highest levels. However, a personal brand that ignites people, mobilizes them into action and influences public opinion is what's even more special.

Do you know who William Dawes was? Like Paul Revere, Dawes was assigned the task of letting Boston's neighboring towns know, "The Redcoats are coming! The Redcoats are coming!" Revere went north; Dawes went west at exactly the same time, in exactly the same way—by horse—and with exactly the same message. Both men covered the same number of towns over an equal number of miles. And yet Revere's presence alerted the militia and ignited the passion of his countrymen. Dawes' efforts, on the other hand, did little to rouse the people.

Revere went down as arguably America's greatest sentinel. Dawes disappeared into anonymity. Why? Because if you look at Paul Revere's background, he had a more compelling personal brand than William Dawes had and, thus, more credibility with the public.

As recounted by Malcolm Gladwell in his *New York Times* bestseller, *The Tipping Point*, Paul Revere's personal brand was the *consummate connector*. Revere was ". . . gregarious, intensely social. When he died, his funeral was attended, in the words of one contemporary newspaper account, by a 'troop of people.'"

Fast-forward to 2006. Personal branding is as relevant today as it was back in 1775. We have the advent of the "celebrity CEO"—Jack Welch, Ken Lay, Hank Greenberg—pop stars like Britney Spears who can't sing very well and yet manage to produce multi-platinum CDs. We even have people who are famous just for being famous—such as Paris Hilton, Donald Trump and Simon Cowell.

Financial success and celebrity status with your target audience are greatly influenced by how compelling your personal brand is. Think about it: How often have you seen one of your competitors with less talent and knowledge than you win a client, job promotion or other opportunity that should have gone to you? If you look closely you will probably see that, while you are laboring away behind your desk, this competitor is out there selling himself to *your* target audience. His primary focus is on promoting himself and his personal brand because he knows he can always find someone to do the work.

Effort earns you calluses. Likeability and visibility bring you riches, access, influence and freedom. I haven't discovered anything new here. William Shakespeare wrote all about it in the late 1600s: "What is most important is a reputation and name."

The people who control their own destinies and drive positive change in their communities are the ones with the best personal brand. If you are a professional who hopes to build a multimillion-dollar book of business, an executive who wants to be CEO of his company or a politician trying to get elected to higher office, heed this advice: He who has the most likeable personal brand has the best chance of winning.

Through this book you will gain an understanding of what exactly a personal brand is, why a personal brand is essential to your success and the five critical steps you need to follow in order to build your own compelling personal brand. My commitment to you is to give you everything you need to build the Lance Armstrong, Oprah Winfrey or Rudy Giuliani brand in your business.

The magic, however, is in the doing. Many will pick this book up. Some will flip through its pages. Several will read it cover to cover. But only a select few will actually do the work. As it says in Corinthians 9:24-27: "Do you not know that those who run in a race all run, but only one receives the prize? Run in such a way that you may win."

My question to you is: Will you run to win?

Part
ONE

Why Personal Branding Is Critical Today

ONE

It *Is* All About You . . .

When someone meets us for the first time, here are the facts:

- In one-quarter of one second, a person makes up his or her mind about us.
- In the first five seconds, a person's first impression of us will flip back and forth 11 times.
- A person's first impression is more important than his or her next five combined.

The message? We are the product—*and* our fate could be sealed before we utter a single word.

The great motivational speaker Napoleon Hill summed it up perfectly: "People buy personality and ideas long before they buy products and services." The same sentiment was echoed by Harry Beckwith in his bestselling book *What Clients Love*. Beckwith reports that statistics overwhelmingly show that most people buy the person first, company second, products/services third and price last. Not surprisingly, Beckwith also found that most of us sell in exactly the reverse order: price first, products/services second, company third and ourselves last.

What all this means is that how we present *ourselves* is more important than price, product and, yes, even smarts. And the most effective way to package *ourselves* is to create a compelling personal brand.

What Exactly Is a Personal Brand?

One of the best definitions of a personal brand I've come across is by a colleague of mine, Peter Montoya. In his terrific book *The Personal Branding Phenomenon*, Montoya defines a personal brand as "a personal identity that stimulates a meaningful emotional response in another person or audience about the qualities or values for which a person stands."

In layman's terms, a personal brand is the *word* or *phrase* we want others to think of when they think of us. For example, when you think of Bruce Springsteen, what word or phrase comes to mind? *The Boss?* What about Tom Hanks? *The nicest guy in the world?* How about Laura Bush? *A classy lady?* What about the *go-to* person in your industry? What word or phrase comes to mind when you think of that individual? How would you like to command the same degree of respect and influence with your target audience? The key to achieving such success is building a great personal brand and marketing that brand better than your competition.

There are three important parts to a personal brand that we must bear in mind if we hope to create a compelling brand of our own. First, our personal brand is our *personal identity*. Second, it must *stimulate a meaningful emotional response*. Third, our personal brand must be the embodiment of the specific *value and quality for which we want to stand*.

1. *Personal Identity*

One of the forums we use at The Personal Branding Group, Inc., to help our clients create celebrity status within their industry is our Rainmaker U. program. In Rainmaker U., we teach professionals earning $200,000 or more per year how to position themselves as *The Person to See*™ in their business by helping them crystallize their personal brand and market that brand better than their competition. Whenever I ask a class to give me their definition of a personal brand, they almost always say, "It's my identity." Technically, that is correct. Our brand is our personal identity; it reflects who we are and how our target audience perceives us.

Therefore, the personal brand we choose for ourselves should be connected to a part of our character upon which we want to build our personal identity. The goal in selecting our personal brand is to discover the strongest and most appealing aspect of our character and then promote that part of us until we become the embodiment of that trait.

Conversely, a personal brand should never be expressed in terms of our profession or craft. This is because our personal brand far transcends what we do for a living. Our profession just happens to be the forum in which our personal brand is expressed. For example, a lawyer's personal brand should never be *great lawyer*. A mortgage broker is never the *best mortgage broker*. And an insurance salesman is never an *incredible insurance broker*.

A friend of mine, Sean Howard, recently shared a story with me that illustrates this point perfectly. Sean works with Brett Favre's agent, James "BVS" Cook Jr. A few months after the 2004 season, Sean and James went to visit Brett at his 450-acre home in Hattiesburg, Mississippi. As they arrived at Brett's house, they made a left and traveled up the driveway, until they happened upon Brett's wife, Deanna, who was outside playing with the kids.

"Hi, Deanna. Where's Brett?" James called from the car.

"In the barn," Deanna responded. "Go on back."

Sean and James parked, got out of the car and walked around the back of the house, unannounced, into the cavernous structure, and, there, bent over, working on the motor of an old, beat-up tractor was three-time MVP Brett Favre.

"Hey, Brett!" James called.

Surprised, Brett looked up and smiled. "What are you all doing here?"

"We came to see you," James responded with a grin.

Sean was absolutely stunned to see this multimillionaire wearing an old T-shirt, covered in grease, fretting over repairing an engine that he could have easily replaced without making a dent in his petty cash account.

What else did he expect from the *toughest* quarterback in the NFL? Whether he is playing in frigid conditions at Lambeau Field, at home working on his tractors or hunting with his buddies, Brett's personal brand remains the same: He is the epitome of *tough*.

Colin Powell is another prime example of someone whose personal brand is so much more than what he does for a living. In 1983, Colin Powell emerged onto the national stage when he was appointed by President Ronald Reagan to lead the National Security Agency. Powell subsequently served as the Chairman of the Joint Chiefs of Staff in the first Bush Administration. Finally, in 2000, Powell was called back into public service when he was appointed by President George W. Bush to serve as Secretary of State. Powell was able to move from position to position largely because of the power of his personal brand, which in my mind is *integrity*. Few would argue with the statement that "when you look up the definition of *integrity* in the dictionary, you will find a picture of Colin Powell."

It was no coincidence that President Bush selected Secretary of State Powell to make the United States' case before the United Nations for invading Iraq in order to disarm Saddam Hussein. Bush could have made the case himself in a nationally televised statement. He could have chosen Vice President Dick Cheney to appear on his behalf. He could even have allowed the U.S. Ambassador to the United Nations at the time, John Negroponte, to make the case. But instead, President Bush and his advisors chose Secretary Powell precisely because Powell's personal brand of *integrity* would add credibility to the supporting evidence.

When selecting our personal brand, we may decide that we want it to relate to an aspect of our physicality. For example, Shaq is known as *The Diesel*, Arnold Schwarzenegger is *The Terminator* and Verne Troyer, *Mini Me*.

Maybe we want to highlight our brains and intellect. Former President Clinton is hailed for his *political savvy*. Albert Einstein was the *absent-minded genius*. With his degree in nuclear engineering, Jimmy Carter is regarded by many as the *smartest U.S. president* in modern times.

Some play up a feature of their personality. Dennis Rodman is *outrageous*. Jerry Garcia of the Grateful Dead was a *free spirit*. Political pundit Ann Coulter is *antagonistic*.

Whatever part of our character we decide to promote, there is one golden rule we can never violate if we hope to have a great personal brand: We must never try to be something we are not. Our personal brand must at all times be a true reflection of who we are.

I was reading Jack Welch's book *Jack: Straight from the Gut*, wherein Welch recounted a story about his first General Electric Board of Directors meeting after being made Vice Chairman at the age of 42. Up to that point in his career, Welch had been regarded by his colleagues as unpolished and abrasive. He also had a funny-sounding voice that was accented by a pronounced lisp. Not exactly leading-man credentials. Welch was determined to change others' perceptions of him.

At this first board meeting as Vice Chairman, he came dressed uncharacteristically in an immaculately fitted blue suit, crisp white shirt and bold red tie. During the meeting, he chose his words carefully, agreeing as much as possible with the other Board members. Welch was determined to fit in.

Midway through the meeting, the Board took a coffee break. Paul Austin, a fellow Board member who was also the Chairman of Coca-Cola, approached Welch and offered some advice, which Welch took to heart. "Jack," Austin said, "you are not being you. You are much better when you are just being yourself."

Welch vowed that, from that point forward, he would never again pretend to be something he was not.

Not everyone can be Brad Pitt or Julia Roberts. Some of us have to be *Pee-wee Herman, Charlie Hustle* or *Urkel*. And this ain't so bad. Think about it. Paul Reubens became a star and made a lot of money being Pee-wee Herman before he screwed it all up by getting arrested for indecent exposure. Pete Rose made millions and became a national role model with the unglamorous personal brand of *Charlie Hustle,* only to squander it all by betting on baseball and then lying about it to the public. Urkel? I couldn't tell you where he is, but I bet he's awfully rich and has the freedom to do what he wants, when he wants, with whom he wants.

Let me share a story with you about a client of mine, David Griffin, who struggled mightily with this issue of authenticity. David is an outstanding residential title insurance broker in Los Angeles. He is an absolutely awesome person. David's got just about all the natural gifts one could wish for. He is 6'2", good looking, smart, has a great personality and is a first-class family man. I love and admire him and try to emulate many of the qualities he possesses.

When David and I started working together on his personal brand, he gravitated toward more sexy and glamorous descriptive words and phrases. David is by no means full of himself. It's just that he wanted a personal brand that really sounded good to him personally and, at the same time, would wow his target audience. The problem we kept running up against when examining David's words and phrases was, while they may have sounded good, they were not relevant to the needs of his target audience.

After David and I drilled down further, using a unique process created to help clients identify the right personal brand for themselves,

I suggested to David that the word or phrase I thought best reflected him and that would also resonate with his target audience was *reliable.*[1] When I initially shared my opinion with David, I thought he was going to pass out. *"Reliable?!"* he repeated in utter disbelief. "I don't want to be reliable!" he protested. "That's boring."

After we had a few laughs over my selection, I explained to David why I thought *reliable* was the right personal brand for him.

First, I asked, "David, is title insurance a glamorous profession?"

"No," he acknowledged.

I then asked, "Is title insurance important in the process of closing a residential real estate transaction?"

"Absolutely," he said.

"Do real estate agents want to get involved in closing title to a property?" I queried further.

"Heck no!" he said.

"What do agents want when it comes to closing title?" I asked.

David responded, "Just that it is closed and they don't have any-thing to worry about, period."

"In other words," I said, "all they want is the peace of mind that comes with knowing that when David Griffin is working on their transaction, everything will be taken care of. That they can rely on you. No?"

"I hate you," he said, smiling.

"You are the embodiment of *reliability*, David," I said. "You are *Mr. Reliable.*"

Over the next 12 months, David and I continued to play with dozens of descriptive words and phrases that still embodied the char-acteristic of *reliability*, but also excited David more than *Mr. Reliable* did. We finally agreed on *The guy gets the job done* as the phrase he would like people to think of when they think of him.

---

1. In Chapter Nine, Building Your Own Personal Brand, I will take you through the same process I took David through so that you can also identify your personal brand.

The key to the process David and I went through was coming up with a word or phrase that accurately reflected a part of David's character that was also relevant to his target audience. Once we had agreed upon the core or essence of David's personal brand, we were free to play around with a lot of words and phrases until we hit upon the one that excited David the most. Today, David is the number three broker in his company, and in the top 5 percent of all residential title insurance brokers nationally.

I have another dynamite client who had hoped to one day become the largest landowner in America. When we first met, he was 30 years old. He owned some investment property, but most of his wealth was created by his extremely successful residential mortgage brokerage business. As this client worked through the same process as David and I had, his initial stab at his personal brand was *Young Real Estate Tycoon.* On one level, this made perfect sense. A young real estate tycoon is what he aspired to be. However, he was not one when we met.

After doing some brainstorming together, I asked him point-blank, "What is the one thing you do better than all your competitors?"

Without hesitation he shot back, "I out-hustle everyone."

"Bingo!" I said. "That's your personal brand: *The guy out-hustles everyone.*"

"I *out-hustle* everyone?" he quietly repeated to himself a few times, letting it sink in a little bit deeper with each recitation.

This client no longer has the ambition to be the largest landowner in America, but he certainly hasn't stopped out-hustling everyone. He has gone on to create an incredible CD and workbook program called "7 Steps to a 720," which helps consumers turn their credit around in just a few months. He has also recently struck a distribution deal with Nightingale-Conant that could potentially generate millions of dollars in passive income for him. And all he did to create this money-making machine was take an idea, *hustle* to learn what he needed to know to credential himself as an expert, *hustle* to package it and *hustle* to find someone to help him spread the gospel of his product and personal brand.

2. *Must Stimulate Meaningful Emotional Response*

Our personal brand won't do us much good if it does not evoke strong, positive emotions in the hearts of our target audience. Tiger Woods, Oprah Winfrey and Michael Jordan inspire us to be our best.

George Foreman, Terry Bradshaw and John Madden are lovable personalities who make us laugh and feel good. FDR, Ronald Reagan and Winston Churchill were strong leaders who had the courage to stand up to bullies.

In addition to thinking about the identity we want to project, we should be asking ourselves, "How do I want to make others feel?" Happy? Motivated? Inspired? How people feel about us is so much more important than what we think about ourselves. When our personal brand is able to influence how people feel, we will be able to lead them where we want them to go, as well as drive positive change in the world.

We need look no further than the words of Winston Churchill and Martin Luther King Jr. to appreciate how powerful the ability to stir up emotions can be. Sir Winston literally carried the free world on his back in the early stages of World War II on the strength of his personal brand. With his "We must never, ever give up" speech, he inspired the world to go on when all seemed hopeless. One of Churchill's aides once remarked, "He possesses that one great quality that all great leaders have, the ability to pass on to those around him something of himself, his courage, his stamina, his great will."

I well up every time I hear Martin Luther King's incomparable "I have a dream" and "I've been to the mountaintop" rallying cries. King's words are the most powerful I have ever heard. Because of the towering impact of his words, he was indeed able to move mountains.

In order for us to get people emotional about what we do, we must give them something to get emotional about. Maybe it is the way we live on a daily basis or the adversity we've overcome.

I remember Gail Devers' triumph in the 1992 Summer Olympics in Barcelona, Spain. Gail is a world-class sprinter who had dominated numerous track and field events around the world in the years leading up to the '92 Games. Then, suddenly, without a hint or warning, her world came crashing down.

Not feeling well several months before the Olympic Games, Gail went to her doctor for a checkup. She was stunned to learn that she had been afflicted with Graves Disease, a potentially terminal illness. Gail's doctor informed Gail that her condition would end her hopes of competing in the Olympics. Her doctor also cautioned that if Gail did not take care of herself, she might have to have her feet amputated.

Where the average competitor would have quit, Gail powered on, vowing to compete in the '92 Games. And compete she did.

All eyes were upon her on the opening night of the competition, her backstory too irresistible for the press to overlook. Her first race was the 110-meter hurdles.

As the starting gun sounded, Gail exploded out of the blocks, taking an early lead. The crowd roared with delight. The race would be over in less than 13 seconds, Gail defying the odds and being coronated one of the fastest women in the world. But on that night it was not to be. As Gail leapt over the last hurdle, the tip of her right toe caught the top of the hurdle, causing her to trip and fall.

The slow-motion cameras caught every painful moment as Gail crawled over the finish line in last place. The reporters all rushed to the track in hopes of being the first to find out from Gail what happened and how she felt.

I remember as if it were yesterday how Gail responded to one reporter's ill-timed question. Shoving his microphone in her face, the reporter asked, "Gail, how do you feel?"

I am sure Gail shocked more than a few people when she broke into a wide smile and said, "I feel great!"

Perplexed by her optimism, the reporter followed up. "Gail, how can you possibly feel great? You just came in last place in a race you were supposed to have won."

Not missing a beat, Gail uttered these inspiring words, "Tonight, the whole world knew I was the best. I just tripped and fell. I've got to just pick myself up and go on." And on she went, winning three medals (two gold and one silver) before the Games came to an end.

For her courage, her ability to persevere and her refusal to allow self-pity to overtake her, Gail Devers was the darling of those '92 Olympic Games and her personal brand will be immortalized in the annals of the Olympic track and field games.

With all the examples of superstars with nationally recognized personal brands, you might be thinking to yourself, "Tim, this all sounds well and good, but how does personal branding apply to me? I'm not now, and probably never will be, famous." Be assured that personal branding applies to your life and mine as much as it does to Lance Armstrong's, Tom Cruise's and Hillary Clinton's.

We do not have to have a personal brand that commands the attention of the national press or the world stage in order to inspire people to have powerful, positive feelings about us. All we need to focus on is our target audience. Think and act locally. I have legions of friends and clients who are not on the national stage who have built great personal brands that inspire an outpouring of powerful, positive emotions.

One client of mine in particular, Robert Brunswick, comes to mind. Robert is the President and CEO of Buchanan Street Partners, a top-flight real estate banking investment firm in Newport Beach, California. In 2005, Robert was recognized as Orange County's Entrepreneur of the Year as part of an annual competition sponsored by Ernst & Young. While certainly very bright, Robert will be the first to tell you that earning this honor had little to do with how smart he is. He is also quick to point out that a large number of people at Buchanan Street contributed to his earning this distinction as much as he did. What Robert will also downplay is the role his personal brand had in getting Buchanan Street to achieve such meteoric success in just seven short years of existence.

Robert's personal brand is *success*. He has been a success his whole life in everything he's done. People love to be around him and play on his team, hoping to be swept up in his next big wave of success. Robert has that extraordinarily rare power to enroll people in a shared vision and inspire them to be better.

Sometimes people fail to realize that a great personal brand does not drive circumstances, as much as circumstances create opportunity for great brands to shine. George W. Bush is an excellent example. Due to the controversy of the 2000 election, George W. Bush's presidency got off to a slow start, to say the least. Many questioned his credibility as president, as well as his professional capability to get the job done. As a consequence, President Bush's personal brand was on life support in the early stages of his first term. That all changed on 9/11. Even his harshest critics had to acknowledge that George Bush rose to the occasion in the aftermath of 9/11. His style and personal brand were exactly what we, as a nation, needed at that moment.

Of course, reasonable minds can differ on the wisdom of his policies in the ensuing years. But when George Bush stood atop the rubble at Ground Zero and bellowed through a bullhorn, "Well, I can hear you and soon the whole world will hear you," he embodied what we all felt collectively as a nation.

The same can be said of Rudy Giuliani. As late as September 10, 2001, a great portion of the New York electorate was prepared to burn Giuliani in effigy. His edgy, in-your-face leadership style had grown old. Much of New York City was ready for a change.

Again, the terrorist attacks of 9/11 created the world stage and Giuliani's personal brand was the right one for the times. No human could have faked the courage he displayed on the morning of September 11. Without regard for his own well-being, Giuliani headed south, straight for Ground Zero, while at the same time exhorting people to head north away from the danger. In the early hours of hysteria, Giuliani revealed himself to be an authentic *leader.* Because of the way he made us feel on that day, Giuliani immortalized himself—not just as New York City's mayor, but as the world's mayor as well.

3. Values and Qualities for Which to Stand

The third key element of our personal brand is that it must stand for a very specific set of values or qualities.

One of my favorite quotes is: "Stand for something special and the crowd will follow you. Stand for nothing and you will spend your whole life following the crowd." I don't know who said it, but it sure is true. Before people will become emotionally attached to us and our brand, they must know what we stand for. We've all heard the saying, "When it comes to so-and-so, what you see is what you get." Before people buy *us,* they want to know what it is they will be getting.

Do you know why John Hancock signed his signature as large as he did? So the king could read it without his spectacles. John Hancock wanted there to be no doubt about where he stood on the issue of America's independence.

Our personal brand is our *promise* to people about what they can expect from us in the way of results. It's why people pay to see Lebron James play, Meryl Streep act and Mikhail Gorbachev speak. If we fail to deliver on the promise people have come to expect from us, our audiences will quickly vanish.

Movie stars in Hollywood are a prime example. Jim Carrey exploded onto the scene in *Ace Ventura: Pet Detective.* In his role as Ace, Carrey played a lovable, zany character. When he played similar characters in *The Mask* and *Liar Liar,* Carrey was a big hit. We loved him because he was exactly who we expected him to be. But when he deviated from this lovable, zany character type, his movies flopped. A small sampling of those cinematic duds is *The Cable Guy, The Truman Show* and *Me, Myself & Irene.*

The same thing happened to Eddie Murphy. We loved him and his caustic wit in such memorable films as *Beverly Hills Cop, Trading Places* and *Coming to America.* He was also brilliant in his HBO Special, *Raw.* Once his fame started going to his head, Eddie Murphy began to fancy himself a sex symbol and professional singer. When he changed his promise, people turned him off *and* tuned him out.

Driven by ego, Eddie Murphy released his own album, *How Could It Be,* which bombed. He has also starred in some real doozies, such as *The Distinguished Gentleman* and *Vampire in Brooklyn,* all of which deviated from the character type we had come to love and expect him to play.

Lately, Eddie Murphy has reconnected with his audience by once again giving us the original Eddie in such recent hits as *The Nutty Professor* and *Bowfinger.* Because his original promise was so awesome, his audience has welcomed him back with open arms.

I suspect that Jim Carrey and Eddie Murphy were bewildered by their respective audiences' reactions. After all, they were only trying to expand their theatrical ranges. It doesn't matter how sincere their efforts may have been; Jim Carrey and Eddie Murphy failed in their forays into new territories because they did not deliver on the promises their audiences had come to expect from them.

Start thinking now about what promise you want to deliver to your target audience. Is it *expertise? Perseverance?* Or *trust?* Select carefully because once you pick your promise and build a reputation, it will be very hard to change.

Whatever you choose, remember, you must be authentic. No one likes a phony.

For years I've paid a vendor more than $20,000/year for services he has performed for me and my company. At the inception of our relationship, this vendor represented to me that his personal brand was *he cares about you.* Yet, most of his interaction with me since our initial meeting has contradicted his promise.

He has told me on more than one occasion that I am one of his most "valued" clients, and yet every year I get preprinted holiday cards addressed, "Dear Timothy." No one who knows me calls me Timothy. Additionally, these cards are either not signed at all or the signature is professionally printed.

The only time I hear from this vendor is when it is time to sell me more services. All of this would be irrelevant, except for the fact that he sold me on the promise that he was different because *he cared about me.* Don't make the mistake of telling people what they want to hear. Have the guts to be you.

I remember one of the last cases I worked on as a lawyer before I left the practice to build my current company. The case involved a group of 20 affluent businessmen from Orange County, California, who were interviewing law firms about a class-action securities lawsuit they wanted to file against a well-known Fortune 500 company and one of the major securities houses.

My boss at the time was a very prominent lawyer in Los Angeles. Getting this case would have been a real feather in his cap for several reasons: (1) It would have meant that he beat out a number of prominent local Orange County firms, (2) the damages in the case were potentially in excess of $100 million and (3) winning the case would go a long way toward putting him and his firm on the map as securities experts. Because the stakes were high, it would have been understandable if my boss had gone into the presentation and said whatever it took to win the dog and pony show. To his credit, that is exactly what he did not do.

Right out of the gate, my boss made clear what these businessmen could expect from him. I am sure he shocked just about everyone in the room, including me, when he said, "Before we go any further, I want to be perfectly clear about one thing. If you expect to be able to talk to me on a daily basis about issues on your case, I'm not your man. My two associates [referring to me and another associate who was also at the meeting] will be available whenever you need them.

You are hiring me for one reason: to try your case." And then he went silent.

For what seemed like an eternity, no one spoke. Then one of the businessmen broke the silence with a solemn, "We understand, continue." My boss finished up his presentation and left the meeting. By 4:00 p.m. that afternoon, he had been retained to represent these businessmen.

The point I am trying to make is, the real power lies in our having the courage to stand for values or qualities that truly reflect who we are as opposed to who we think our target audience wants us to be.

Make your promise singular. The best brands are simple, straightforward and unambiguous. John F. Kennedy had *style*. Marilyn Monroe was *sexy*. Margaret Thatcher is the *Iron Lady*. Each of the titans has become synonymous with a single quality or trait.

Pick one thing and be known for that one thing better than anyone else. The objective is to become the epitome of the value or quality. Is there any doubt in your mind that in the dictionary next to the word *winner* is a picture of Tiger Woods or next to the word *courage* is a picture of Nelson Mandela? How about *selfless?* Mother Teresa.

Chapter Summary

Key Points

- Our personal brand should be based upon a part of our humanness, not what we do for a living (e.g., a bulldog vs. a great attorney).
- If your picture were to appear in the dictionary as the definition of a quality, what would you want that quality to be? (e.g., competitive, innovative, charismatic)
- Make your personal brand singular and unambiguous (e.g., Brett Favre is tough).

It's Not What *You Think,* but How *Others Feel* That Matters

The single most important step in building a great personal brand is accepting the fact that what we think of ourselves is essentially irrelevant; personal branding is all about what *others feel* about us.

I recently read an article in the *San Jose Mercury News* that recounted a comment Stanley Marcus, son of one of the founders of Neiman Marcus, made to Tim Sanders, author of *Love Is the Killer App*. Sanders was interviewing Mr. Marcus as part of his research for his book. As Sanders got up to leave, Mr. Marcus offered him these parting words, "Son, don't forget one thing: Make yourself emotionally attractive. Good things happen to those who are emotionally attractive."

Al Ries and his daughter Laura, authors of *The Origin of Brands*, define the process of branding as "reserving a word or phrase in the mind of another." The word or phrase we choose for ourselves should in some way reflect the emotions we want to evoke in our target audiences.

Take Mercedes. Mercedes wants their clients to *feel special.* The word it wants others to associate with its products is *prestige.* All of Mercedes' products, customer service and advertising are targeted toward reserving the word *prestige* in the minds of its target audience.

27

Starbucks is another great example of making people feel special. I once heard someone say, "Starbucks not only markets its coffee with its distinctive cup and expensively priced coffee, but the coffee drinker as well. People who walk around holding their Starbucks coffee cup for all to see are making their own personal statement: 'See, I can afford to pay more for my coffee. I'm part of an elite club.'"

The process is the same when it comes to personal branding. Think feelings. Others'—not your own.

Emotions move people to action, and no one knows this better than the National Football League. The NFL's public relations machine is awesome at promoting the personal brands of its players. Let's examine the personal brand of one of the NFL's biggest stars, Peyton Manning. Manning is beloved by players, coaches and fans alike. Why? Because he makes us *feel* good when we watch him play. This emotional capital also translates into very lucrative endorsement deals for Manning.

Peyton's personal brand got off to a faster start than most because he was fortunate to have had a foil to play off of, by the name of Ryan Leaf. In 1998, the Indianapolis Colts had the first pick in the draft. The San Diego Chargers had the second pick. All the way up to the actual moment of announcement, no one knew whom the Colts would pick first, Manning or Leaf. The good kid, begotten from the genes of NFL Hall of Fame legend Archie Manning, or the off-the-charts raw talent who also had a wild streak? The Colts made the safe choice and went with Manning. The Chargers chose Leaf.

The good kid turned out to be a great kid who reported to training camp early, worked night and day to learn the Colts' complex offensive system and struggled through a dismal 3 and 13 rookie season that included being sacked 22 times without so much as a peep of poor sportsmanship. Today, few would doubt that Manning's destiny is the NFL Hall of Fame.

In contrast, Ryan Leaf imploded almost from the moment he was drafted. After being given a $31.25 million, four-year contract, he proceeded to alienate teammates, insult the press and engage in foulmouthed tirades toward fans; he even went so far as to threaten physical violence against a few of them. Leaf's personal brand quickly became *bust*. Things with Ryan Leaf got so bad, the Chargers eventually ate the remainder of Leaf's contract and cut him after three years of torture. Leaf subsequently bounced around the League for awhile until retiring ignominiously in 2002.

Even to this day, few scouts would argue that Ryan Leaf had more raw talent than Peyton Manning, but Manning had the discipline to create a more likeable and reliable personal brand.

How people feel about us is equally important when it comes to how the public votes in elections. I submit that the 2004 presidential election was not decided by policy preferences, but rather by personal brand appeal. And President Bush won, not so much because he successfully branded himself as a *leader,* but more so because he successfully branded Senator John Kerry as a *flip-flopper.*

The very real threat of another terrorist attack on American soil intensified the importance of the issue of leadership in the race between President Bush and Senator Kerry. Since 9/11, President Bush has worked assiduously to brand himself as a leader, making tough-talking speeches, emphasizing the need to do what it takes to protect America, arriving by a Navy S-3B Viking jet on the deck of an aircraft carrier, making a surprise visit to the troops in Iraq despite the threat of death.

By the time the race began in earnest between the president and Kerry on September 4, President Bush was recognized in all the polls as a strong leader, whether you liked him or not. Senator Kerry knew the leadership issue was a mountain he would have to surmount if he hoped to win on November 2.

Senator Kerry came out with guns blazing at the Democratic Convention, delivering the memorable line, "John Kerry reporting for duty." Everything Senator Kerry did in the aftermath of the convention was designed to reinforce his record as a decorated war hero, a true leader of men in combat. Senator Kerry's leadership numbers instantly went up in the polls.

The Republicans knew if they were to hold their lead, they would have to be ready to challenge Senator Kerry on his leadership credentials. Day in and day out, they attacked the credibility of Senator Kerry's record as a war hero with blistering TV commercials (e.g., the Swift Boat ads), until they were able to put Senator Kerry on the defensive.

At the same time the Republicans attacked his war record, they also pounded Senator Kerry from another flank, accusing him of being a flip-flopper on the tough issues. No matter how hard he tried, Senator Kerry could not shake free from his infamous, "I actually voted for the $87 billion package before I voted against it" line.

When it came down to the wire, the Republicans had done a better job branding Senator Kerry than Senator Kerry had done branding himself. The policies of the candidates were rendered all but irrelevant because of the stark contrast in personal brands. In the end, the people wanted a president who they *felt* would be best able to protect them. The personal brand of George Bush was the safer choice.

When selecting our personal brand, we must look at ourselves through the eyes of our target audience and never lose sight of what *they* see and how what they see makes them *feel* about us. This is an easy principle to acknowledge, but a very hard one for most of us to practice. When it comes to personal branding and making an honest assessment of who we really are, many of us have a tendency to think more highly of ourselves than we probably should. The results of two studies deftly illustrate my point.

Not too long ago, I was reading an article in *Men's Health* magazine that talked about how some men sometimes have an inflated perception of themselves. A random sample of several hundred men was asked to respond to the following question: "Do you think you are good looking?"

Based upon the responses of those polled, the survey facilitators were able to extrapolate that 80 percent of all men think they are "*very* good looking"! Could be a tad bit high, no ladies?

I also read an article in *Time* magazine on obesity. Again, a random sampling of Americans was asked to respond, this time to the question: "Do you think you are overweight?" Extrapolating from those surveyed, the pollsters were able to calculate that 19.7 percent of Americans believe themselves to be overweight. The truth is that a full 33 percent of Americans are obese!

The problem with an inflated sense of self in our context is, if we are never honest with ourselves we will have a very difficult time identifying the personal brand that is right for us. I urge you to be harder on yourself than others might be.

In our Rainmaker U. program, we use a very straightforward exercise to help our new clients gain some valuable self-perspective before beginning the process of intentionally identifying their personal brand. Our classes are typically made up of a mix of 20 executives, business owners and professionals from 12 to 15 different industries who have come together for the sole purpose of learning how to identify and market their personal brand.

At the beginning of the class, each student receives a stack of 20 3x5 index cards. Each index card has a label with the name of each student printed on it.

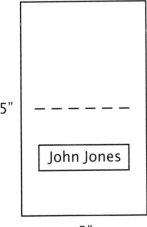

First, we instruct the participants to find the index card with their own name and, on the reverse side, write the word or phrase they believe they are projecting to those around them.

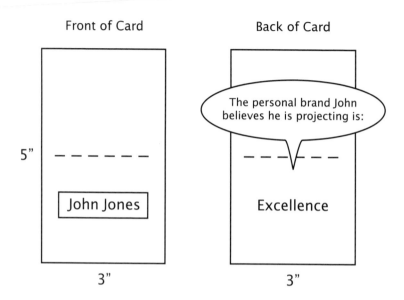

We then instruct everyone to write down on the other 19 index cards their first impressions of everyone else in the class. We remind them that it doesn't matter if they've had any contact with the person or not; our research shows that when meeting someone for the first time, we make up our minds about that person within just one-quarter of one second. The idea is to provide each student in the class with the feedback from 19 strangers who have absolutely no hidden agenda.

All comments remain 100 percent confidential, so we encourage everyone in the class to be brutally honest with their feedback. The only requirement I impose is that if someone does have a negative first impression of another class participant, he must provide an explanation as to why he has that specific feeling. For example, the comment "He's a jerk" means nothing unless the recipient understands why this person formed this impression. Furthermore, if someone came across as a "jerk," I imagine he would want to know exactly why that was, so that he could then make an informed decision about whether or not to change something about himself.

Below is an example of how a participant providing feedback is expected to fill out another participant's card.

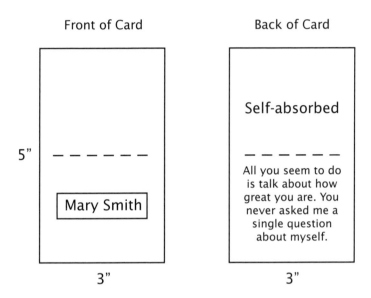

Once everyone has written down their first impressions of everyone else, we collect all of the index cards and sort them by name so that, on the break, the students can read what personal brand they are *actually* projecting to those around them.

This can be a very sobering exercise. It has been my experience that the most successful and driven students are always eager to receive constructive feedback, whether positive or negative. To the open-minded person who is truly dedicated to growth, feedback is never negative. Rather, it's just information to process and perhaps act upon. The best and the brightest know how tough it is to get to the top, so they are always on the lookout for anything new that can help them improve.

On the other hand, there are many students who hold their breath and cringe as they read each card, hoping the feedback isn't too brutal. It matters more to these people that they dodge a bullet than that they receive healthy, constructive feedback, even though it might be negative.

I encourage you to try this exercise yourself, even if you cannot get 20 strangers to fill out index cards. Do it with colleagues who know you. All feedback is valuable.

In Year Two of our program, we take this process much further with our customized 360-degree evaluation tool. Specifically, we have our clients fill out a 10-page survey on themselves. The questions cover five different aspects of their personal brand. The objective is to have each client express, in great detail, what personal brand he thinks he is projecting to others.

After a client has completed his self-evaluation, we ask him to identify four colleagues who know him very well and who would be willing to fill out this same survey. The survey is very detailed and takes about 45 minutes to properly complete, so it is critical that the client chooses people who will invest the time. Once we have the names and addresses of four colleagues, our office sends the survey to them to complete.

When we get back all of a client's evaluations from his colleagues, we combine all of the feedback into one document. We then send that combined analysis to the client for him to compare with his own original responses. For someone who is truly dedicated to building a great personal brand, I can imagine few tools more valuable than this 360-degree evaluation process.

THE CURSE OF PROFESSIONAL ARROGANCE

We have found that the number-one blocker preventing many professionals from developing a really great personal brand is professional arrogance. Professional arrogance is essentially being of the mind that we know all there is to know about our business. No one can teach us anything.

We are constantly reminding our clients that they should hope and pray that every person they meet is smarter than they are so that they can learn something new with each interaction. I can imagine few things worse than being so self-absorbed that we close ourselves off from useful, constructive feedback.

There are two primary reasons professional arrogance emerges: (1) low self-esteem and (2) misplaced self-importance. A professional who exhibits professional arrogance is usually trying to compensate for his sense of inferiority. Despite his successes, deep down he feels that who he is and what he has accomplished are not good enough, so he tries to compensate by projecting that he is more than he actually is.

We all know these people. Instead of letting their track record and reputation speak for themselves, they talk incessantly about how awesome they are. In their mind, everything they do is "the best." I constantly preach to my clients, "Don't tell people you are great—just *be* great!"

The second instance in which professional arrogance commonly cripples personal brand growth is when people confuse self-worth and net worth. This is particularly prevalent among professionals who are high-income earners at an early age—what I call the "400 under 40" crowd. These are professionals who earn at least $400,000 a year before they turn 40 years old. If you earn $400,000 per year or more in America today, you are in the top 7 percent of all income earners in the entire country—pretty heady company.

Unfortunately, many of today's young professionals who attain this stature are not mature enough to handle their success. They use their bank account as a success validator. Since they are doing so well, they figure they know just about all they need to know to do everything they want to do. In their own self-inflated opinion, there are very few things others can teach them. And, if they are to learn something new it must come from someone who earns more than they do.

I ran into one of these folks just yesterday. I was having a conversation with a prospect for Rainmaker U. who epitomized my "400 under 40" principle. This gentleman, let's call him Pete, is a 36-year-old commercial insurance broker in San Diego, California, who consistently earns $300,000 to $400,000 per year. We were introduced by a mutual friend. Per my friend's suggestion, I put in a call to Pete.

After some idle chitchat, Pete asked me to give him an overview of the program. When I finished, his reaction was very telling. "Tim, I don't mean to brag, but I don't really need to learn anything else to help me make more money. I'm already pretty much the best in my field. Everybody in San Diego knows that if you are looking for the best commercial insurance broker in San Diego, I'm the guy to call."

Wow! What do you do with that? I thought to myself.

"Pete," I said, "if you are, in fact, already at the level where you can name your price, pick your clients and have a steady stream of people calling you so that you never have to call others, then our program is certainly not for you."

"Well, that's pretty much me," he said. I nearly fell off my chair. At that point, I politely ended the conversation, saying, "Well, our program is not for everyone."

Now let me tell you about another client who participates in Rainmaker U. who is the polar opposite of Pete. Murad Siam is the founding Managing Director of IDS Real Estate Group, a real estate development firm in downtown Los Angeles. I am confident that Murad makes a lot more money than Pete does. Murad's Rainmaker U. class meets once a quarter. Class starts at 8:30 a.m. sharp at the Jonathan Club in downtown Los Angeles. Murad lives in Chatsworth, California, which is 35 miles from downtown L.A. With L.A. traffic, that's one heck of a commute. But that's no matter for Murad. He is always the *first* one to arrive at class. *Always!* In contrast, the $200,000- and $300,000-a-year folks are chronically late.

Moreover, Murad always comes to class the most prepared person in the room; he takes the most notes and religiously completes all homework assignments in a timely manner. It blew me away that a guy so successful would work so hard. But then again, that's why Murad runs the place and Pete will probably always work for a guy like Murad.

There are two qualities that the Murad Siams of the world possess that average performers lack: They have (1) a sense of urgency and (2) a hunger to learn from others—even if it means hearing some uncomfortable feedback.

Murad once told me, "Tim, I don't come close to applying everything you teach us. But if I can learn one or two key things from others in the class that will improve my personal brand, then the investment cost of your program is a drop in the bucket."

There is no doubt in my mind that Murad is well on his way to positioning himself as *The Person to See*™ with his target audience. I'm merely one of the many resources that will help him get there.

CHAPTER SUMMARY

Key Points

- Personal branding is all about how *others feel* about us and has little to do with what *we think* of ourselves.
- Ask yourself, "What is the feeling I want others to have when they encounter me (e.g., inspired, trust, impressed)?"
- We'd better brand ourselves and intentionally promote that brand or others will do it for us (e.g., Senator Kerry as the *flip-flopper*).
- Beware of the curse of professional arrogance—most of us think our personal brand is much more attractive than it really is.

THREE

Personal Branding Is *Not* Optional

Whether or not to have a personal brand is not a choice—*everyone* has a personal brand. What we do get to choose is whether our personal brand is positive, negative or neutral. And what others decide about us may not always be what we like.

How often are we confronted with the situation where others make incorrect snap judgments about us after just a single brief encounter? This dynamic is called the *Fundamental Attribution Error.* It happens to famous people routinely. A fan asks for an autograph at an extremely inconvenient moment. The star gruffly brushes the fan off. In that fan's eyes, the star is a *jerk.* The truth may be that this star is actually a super nice person who was just caught at a bad moment. Too bad! Fairly or not, people make snap judgments about us all the time based upon incomplete information. It is also true that a person is likely to tell at least 12 other people about his negative experience.

The leaders with the most influential personal brands have always decided for themselves what they want their personal brand to be. They are also very intentional and passionate about promoting their personal brand with their target audience. Michael Jordan is a case in point. There was a very specific strategy behind the transformation of

Michael Jordan the superstar basketball player to Michael Jordan the world-class personal brand.

The catalyst for Jordan's transformation was his agent, David Falk. Falk saw the potential Jordan had as a mega-brand, and together he and Jordan crafted a plan to capitalize on this opportunity. The first point of focus was to dispel any preconceived notions the public may have had that Jordan was just another incredibly gifted African-American basketball player.

One of the first things Jordan changed was the gaudy jewelry he regularly wore in the early years of his career. Basketball fans remember the early photos of Jordan sailing gracefully through the air—with gold necklaces and bracelets flying every which way. He was copying those before him. Then the lightbulb came on: Wearing delicate jewelry while playing an intense, high-contact sport is just silly! All at once the pictures of Jordan wearing flamboyant jewelry disappeared.

Jordan and Falk also decided that Jordan would no longer be interviewed in the locker room after games unless he was fully clothed, almost always wearing a suit and tie. No more images of a half-naked Michael Jordan with a towel wrapped around his waist would be seen on ESPN, Sports Center or the evening sports programs. The objective was (and still is) to project the image of an intelligent, articulate, handsome professional who also happened to be a phenomenal basketball player. The impact of Jordan and Falk's strategy was explosive. Toward the end of Jordan's career, he was earning a paltry $1 million in salary compared to a staggering $40 million in endorsement deals.[1]

If you want to get a glimpse of personal brand management in action in the context of politics, read *Ask Not* by Thurston Clarke, in which the author tries to answer the question of who wrote John F. Kennedy's famous inaugural speech. Was it Kennedy himself or his

---

1. Jordan was actually paid so low in comparison to other players because he committed to honoring the contract he had signed with the Chicago Bulls in 1988. Once Jordan's contract did expire in 1996, he capitalized fully, commanding an extraordinary $30 million per season for the remaining two years of his career with the Bulls.

abled speechwriter Ted Sorensen? While I found Clarke's search for the truth interesting, I was equally intrigued by the degree of attention the Kennedys paid to details that would affect the image JFK would project at the day of his inauguration.

For example, Kennedy was obsessed with his face washing out on black-and-white television, so he spent weeks before the inauguration sunbathing at his family's compound in Palm Beach, Florida. Concerned that his cheeks might also look fat, he carefully adhered to a strict diet. Kennedy also knew that the old guard of Truman and Eisenhower would wear dark, conservative suits and heavy overcoats. In stark contrast, Kennedy wore formal dress (top hat and tails) and thermal underwear so he would not have to manage a cumbersome overcoat. Kennedy's promise was loud and clear: young, new, fresh, vibrant and full of exciting possibilities.

The First Lady was quite skilled at image management as well. Jackie correctly anticipated the dress of the matronly Bess Truman, Mimi Eisenhower and Lady Bird Johnson. All three wore dowdy dresses and heavy furs. Jackie stood out brilliantly in her custom-designed pink pillbox hat and outfit. Together that day, the president-elect and future first lady achieved exactly what they had hoped. The American people fell in love with their personal brand of style and elegance. Wittingly or not, it was on that day the Kennedy entourage planted the first seeds of Camelot.

Here are just a few of the things the father of our country, George Washington, did to cultivate his personal brand:

- Attended the first Continental Congress in full military regalia. He was the only person to do so.
- Attended the second Continental Congress in a custom-built carriage, escorted by 50 horsemen.
- Encouraged others to refer to him as "His Excellency."
- Washington was so concerned about his place in history that he convinced the Continental Congress to hire a bank of

secretaries to transcribe his notes. Eight secretaries worked eight hours a day for two years straight until the project was completed.

- When Washington died, all of his 124 slaves were freed outright. He didn't do this so much out of humanity as he did because he knew history would be watching him.

- At the time of his death, Washington was one of the wealthiest people in the nation. Yet he did not want to be remembered as such; he wanted to be thought of as a war hero and founding father of an emerging nation. So rather than bequeath all of his wealth to one person—which was customary at the time in order to preserve family wealth—Washington spread his fortune out over 23 heirs.

For every great example of smart personal brand management, there are dozens of case studies where things have gone miserably wrong. Few people have squandered their personal brand opportunity like Barry Bonds. Put the steroids allegations aside and this guy is a true superstar. We will be hard-pressed to see another great talent like him come along again in our lifetime. And yet, because he is a *jerk,* he was able to command only $4 million in endorsements in 2004. Compare that with his superstar counterparts in other sports: Tiger Woods, $80 million; Lance Armstrong, $17.5 million; and Shaquille O'Neal, $14 million.

Why the disparity? Two reasons: Barry Bonds is so self-absorbed, he apparently lacks any awareness (or doesn't care) about the negative impact of his antisocial behavior. Second, he has surrounded himself with people who indulge his antics. Bonds does not appear to have an established advisor like Jordan has in David Falk. The bigger our personal brand grows, the more important it is to have a reliable confidant who is not afraid to tell us when we have stepped out of line.

I remember going to a political fundraiser for Governor George Pataki of New York. It was a small dinner party of approximately 20 people at the famous Bel Air Hotel in Bel Air, California. I had the honor of sitting next to the governor for more than an hour during dinner, which afforded me some meaningful dialogue with him.

I asked the governor why he believed he was able to win four consecutive terms as governor of New York, a very significant feat for a state with such a fickle electorate. Even the very popular Mario Cuomo was only able to manage being elected to the governorship three times. Governor Pataki attributed his longevity to never taking himself too seriously and always working hard to stay in touch with the people. He also told me that his staff had unconditional freedom to speak their minds and tell him when he was really screwing up. It didn't matter if you were his press secretary, his wife or a staff intern—everyone had the freedom and indeed was expected to put his or her two cents in.

EVERYONE NEEDS A GREAT PERSONAL BRAND

Anyone whose success depends upon the cooperation of another person must have a great personal brand if he hopes to be successful. For example, a lawyer needs to sell his clients on his capabilities and the judge and jury on the merits of his case. A minister needs to sell his flock on the message of the gospels. A corporate executive must sell himself into a job, raise and promotion. He must also sell himself to his people if he hopes to enroll them in a shared vision.

Eight years ago I was having a conversation with Brian Kabateck, a prominent plaintiff's attorney in Los Angeles, about business and career development. Brian said something that was so poignant, it has stuck with me ever since. We were talking about how many professionals (e.g., lawyers, doctors, accountants, etc.) feel that selling is beneath them and their profession.

Brian summed it up perfectly when he asked somewhat facetiously, "Tim, 50 percent of my job is selling, and do you know what the other 50 percent is?"

"No," I said.

"Selling!" he shot back.

Brian gets it. Even though he is good enough at what he does to obtain multimillion-dollar verdicts and settlements for his clients every year, he knows that his primary job is not lawyering, but rather marketing himself and his firm. Every day Brian is selling to judges and juries, pitching potential clients on the benefits of his firm and persuading referring attorneys to send him clients they cannot service. The list of audiences Brian must sell to, day in and day out, is endless. So what's the result of all this hustle? Brian was recently ranked as one of the Top 40 Rainmaking Lawyers in California by the *Los Angeles Daily Journal.* He was also recognized by his peers as Lawyer of the Year in the *California Lawyer Magazine.*

I can give you a list of dozens of lawyers in Los Angeles who are brilliant, capable and hardworking, and yet who have no business. How could that be, you ask? Because they refuse to confront and embrace the truth: Talent and brains are overrated. Those who can create and market their personal brand are worth their weight in gold. Those who merely rely upon their talent and brains to win over their target audience are rarely as successful as they hope to be.

THE CELEBRITY CEO

Do you know who Jeffrey Immelt, Robert Nardelli and James McNerney are? They are the chairmen of General Electric, Home Depot and 3M respectively. Do you know what they did for a living in 2000? Each was a president of a separate division at General Electric. They had also been identified by their predecessor, Jack Welch, as a potential heir apparent to the GE throne.

In 2000, Welch announced that he would be retiring in 12 months. Welch also went to Immelt, Nardelli and McNerney and told them that he believed each of them had what it took to be his successor. He also informed them that he would be watching each of them closely over the next 12 months, at which time he would pick one of them to be his successor. Talk about pressure!

You can just imagine how intensely each candidate worked on selling and marketing his personal brand over those next 12 months. They all knew Welch would choose the personal brand that best exemplified the GE way, the leader who could inspire and enroll others in a shared vision and, most important to Welch, carry on Welch's legacy.

In the end, Welch chose Jeffrey Immelt because Welch believed that, among other reasons, Immelt had the best personal brand to lead GE in the 21st century. Ironically, Immelt has chosen to build and market a very different kind of personal brand than Jack Welch's.

When Welch took over the company in 1981, he described GE as *a stable tanker.* He was determined not to be just a steward of the status quo. Before he retired, Welch wanted to put his own footprint on GE. He wanted to transform GE into a *speedboat,* with GE dominating each business segment it entered into or getting out of that business altogether, a principle he learned from management guru Peter Drucker.

Welch started off with a bang by laying off excess employees, closing unprofitable businesses and even selling GE's prized $300 million housewares division. Employees, Wall Street and stockholders went nuts. Welch was quickly branded in the corporate and financial world as *Neutron Jack.* Despite the intense criticism, Welch pushed on. He was determined to define for himself what his personal brand would be as opposed to letting the naysayers do it for him. Welch also made several bold acquisitions in the commercial lending and entertainment businesses. Everyone was certain Welch would go down in flames.

Today, GE is unrecognizable compared to what it represented prior to the chairmanship and 20-year reign of *Neutron Jack.* The net result of Welch's moves: (1) Recognition as *Forbes'* "Manager of the Century" (1999). (2) The year before Welch took over the GE chairmanship, GE had $26.8 billion in revenues; the year before he retired, GE had $130 billion in revenues. (3) In 2004 GE was valued at $400 billion, the world's largest corporation, up from 10th largest in the United States only in 1981.

For his efforts, *Neutron Jack* is now hailed as *a great visionary* and *America's Number One CEO*—all because he had the guts to decide for himself what his legacy would be.

Jeffrey Immelt has cut quite a different swath in the six short years he has been GE's Chairman and CEO. Like Welch, Immelt is driven to leave his own mark. Immelt has GE embarking on an ambitious plan to recreate the GE brand yet again, transforming the company into the standard for profitable corporate and environmental partnering. For his efforts, Immelt is being hailed as *The Green CEO*.

The point I want to drive home here is that the importance of personal branding is not confined to only sales situations. Let me say it again: Anyone whose success depends upon the cooperation of another person needs to have a compelling personal brand.

As my next-door neighbor Dick Mercer once said to me, "Tim, no one is a success unless an awful lot of people want that person to be."

Don't you think Coach K of Duke is aware of and promotes his own personal brand? Coach K isn't selling a product or service. He's selling an opportunity—the opportunity to come and play for him and be part of the Duke Basketball experience.

Rick Pitino is doing the same thing at Louisville, as is Tubby Smith at Kentucky. Coach K, Rick Pitino and Tubby Smith all offer prized high school recruits virtually the same thing when it comes to the possibility of winning a national championship, national television exposure and training and development for future NBA stardom. What is unique is each coach's personal brand. Typically, the coach with the most attractive personal brand to the recruit and his family gets that player.

Below is a sampling of professionals for whom personal branding may seem unimportant, as well as my rationale as to why their success, too, depends upon an attractive personal brand:

- **A scientist in a laboratory.** He must have a compelling personal brand for three reasons: (1) He must be able to inspire those who work with him to follow him, (2) he needs to sell the money people (e.g., grants, scholarships, benefactors) on himself and his projects and (3) when he does have a breakthrough, he better be able to sell the results to the media and outside world.

- **A college professor.** She must: (1) have a personal brand that attracts and keeps the attention of her students, (2) sell her colleagues on her scholarship in order to earn tenure and (3) be able to sell the administration on the new subjects she wants to teach.

- **A policeman.** He must: (1) sell himself to the community he patrols in order to gain their support, (2) sell himself to his superiors to earn promotions and (3) sell himself to his colleagues to ensure they support him at crucial times.

- **A doctor.** (1) She must sell herself to her patients so they keep coming back. In the event things don't go as planned, patients won't be so quick to sue for malpractice. Because they trust their doctor, they will take the time to find out the facts first. (2) She must sell herself to her colleagues so they refer her new business.

- **A chief financial officer (CFO).** (1) He must sell himself to his boss so that his numbers can be trusted. (2) If he has ambitions to move up the ladder, he must sell himself to his superiors who make the decisions regarding promotions and raises. (3) He must sell himself to outsiders to the extent that they are making business decisions that rely upon the CFO's numbers (e.g., investment choices).

- **A union leader.** She must: (1) sell herself to her constituency that she is the best person to represent them in negotiations, (2) sell herself and her union's demand to the public in order to gain support and (3) sell herself to management that she is a viable voice for her people.

- **A real estate developer.** He must: (1) sell himself to the banks, proving that he knows what he is doing so that the banks can trust him with their money, (2) sell himself to the planning commission who approves his projects and (3) sell himself to the workers because the more they like him, the harder they will work for him.

I cannot think of a single career, job or profession where a personal brand has no relevance. In the above examples, I deliberately chose professions and jobs that have little or nothing to do with the sale of products and services. And yet, we can clearly see how and why personal branding is very relevant to a person's success in each of these careers.

CHAPTER SUMMARY

Key Points

- Personal branding is *not* optional—everyone has a personal brand.
- What we do get to decide is whether our personal brand is positive, negative or neutral.
- If we properly manage our personal brand, we can get our audience to *feel* just about anything (e.g., JFK and Camelot).
- There is not a career, job or profession where personal brand credibility is not important.

FOUR

The Payoff

Why do all this work to create a compelling personal brand? What does having a great personal brand get you at the end of the day? Here are five benefits that you might find compelling:

- Fame and fortune
- The power to influence
- The ability to drive positive change
- Career security and stability
- The power of pull

FAME AND FORTUNE

Very few things can explode your business overnight. Technology is one; a great personal brand is another. The meteoric rise of golf fans' favorite lefty, Phil Mickelson, is a case in point. Every year, *Sports Illustrated* publishes its list of the top 50 highest-paid athletes. They call it the "Fortunate 50." In *Fame and Fortune 2003*, Mickelson was number 36 on the list. Twelve months later, he shot up a staggering 27 places

51

to number 9, earning a whopping $26,384,823 in 2004! Here is the kicker: Mickelson's talent was responsible for generating just $6,384,823 of the total amount he earned. His personal brand earned him the other $20 million through endorsement deals. Why the explosion?

Up until 2003, Phil Mickelson had been unable to win any of the four major tournaments on the Professional Golf Tour (PGA)—U.S. Open, British Open, Masters, U.S. PGA. He had come so close so often that it was becoming almost too painful to watch. And then in 2004, it happened—Mickelson held on to win the Masters by just one stroke over Ernie Els. The golf world cheered wildly—especially the advertisers.

The financial payoff to Mickelson has been incredible. As a result of that one major victory, Mickelson was able to command an endorsement deal with Callaway for close to $10 million, doubling his old contract with Titleist.

Even though Mickelson won the Masters, he was still not the number one golfer in the world in 2004. Vijay Singh was. Yet Singh's earnings and endorsement deals were not nearly enough to earn him a spot on *Sports Illustrated's* Fortunate 50. Why? Because Vijay's personal brand just doesn't sell like Phil's.

At this point, you might be saying to yourself, "This personal branding stuff is all well and good for Phil Mickelson, but what about me? I'm not a superstar athlete, movie star or famous public figure. I am just selling accounting services or computer software, or am merely the CFO of a privately held, mid-size business in the heart of Topeka, Kansas. How does all this talk about personal branding and celebrity status apply to me?" Rest assured, the impact of having a great personal brand is equally important to you and me and our businesses, even if it is not as scalable as Phil Mickelson's, Jack Welch's or Oprah Winfrey's.

I would hazard a guess that quite a few of the people in your industry who make the most money are not necessarily the most technically competent. It certainly is the case in my field, but what these stars lack in technical competency, they more than make up for in personal brand appeal.

I know of one trial attorney in Orange County, California, who makes literally millions of dollars a year and, to tell you the truth, if I were in a pinch I would *never* have him represent me in court. It's not that he's incompetent. It's just that he is nothing special.

And yet, despite his modest skill level, clients flock to him all because he has built a personal brand as a *winner*. In reality, his partner and two associates who handle all the cases are the ones responsible for the wins.

But the truth doesn't matter because his partner's and associates' personal brand appeal is a shadow of their boss. The bottom line is: A little bit of success and a great personal brand will usually go a lot farther than a great track record and minimal personal brand appeal.

HOW INFLUENTIAL ARE YOU?

For proof that a personal brand can influence behavior on a massive scale, we need look no further than Katie Couric. The influential power of her personal brand is unparalleled amongst her peers. Katie may not be the most technically competent or talented anchor on television, but when she underwent a live colonoscopy on morning television in order to raise cancer awareness among her viewership, according to a study done by the University of Michigan, the number of colonoscopies went up 20 percent in the following week! This phenomenon has come to be known as "The Couric Effect." This is exactly why CBS is taking a chance on Katie.[1]

Perhaps you were watching when Jay Leno and Katie switched shows for a day. When Katie sat in for Jay on *The Tonight Show,* its ratings went up 12 percent. *The Today Show*'s ratings with Jay Leno at the helm went up just 4 percent.

---

1. It will be interesting to see if Katie's personal brand of cute will be enough to revive the *CBS Evening News.* The question is, does Katie's personal brand match her targeted audience's needs?

If you think Katie's appeal is overrated and that her superstar status is due to the genius of the show's programming, then why did Deborah Norville and Willow Bay, Katie's two predecessors, fail so miserably?

Katie is a star for two reasons. First, her personal brand is unambiguous and compelling. Katie Couric is the epitome of *cute*. She is the girl next door and America loves the girl next door. Just ask Sandra Bullock, Ashley Judd and Danica Patrick.

The second reason Katie's a star is she has built up a mountain of personal brand equity. Katie's secret is never taking herself too seriously. She's not above dressing up in silly costumes on Halloween (last year she was Marilyn Monroe) or playing along with a guest's stunt that is guaranteed to make Katie look foolish.

Perhaps the biggest deposit Katie made to her personal brand equity bank account was when she courageously came back to *The Today Show* just a couple of weeks after losing her husband, Jay Monahan, to colon cancer. When Katie lost Jay, it was as if our own sister had lost her husband. All of America grieved along with her.

Aside from the universal adulation of her fans, Katie has been rewarded with the highest salary of any television news anchor—$15 million per year. This included anchors Peter Jennings of ABC, NBC's Tom Brokaw, and Dan Rather of the *CBS Evening News,* at their respective peaks.

So what is influence? Influence is the ability to move people from point A to point B. Harry Truman once said, "Influence is the ability to get people to do things they don't want to do and like it." No one likes to undergo a colonoscopy, but I bet most people are glad they have once they are finished, especially if they receive good news.

We know our personal brand is influential when others take action solely because we did or because we recommended they do. How many of us would love to have the power to move people to action like the great American Civil War General Robert E. Lee did?

On more than one occasion, evangelist Billy Graham has recounted the following story that supposedly occurred right after the Civil War:

A negro entered a fashionable church in Richmond, Virginia, on Sunday morning when communion was being served. He walked down the aisle and knelt at the altar. A rustle of shock and anger swept through the congregation. Sensing the situation, a distinguished layman immediately stood up, stepped forward to the altar and knelt beside his brother. Captured by this man's spirit, the congregation followed his magnanimous example. The layman who set the example and moved people to action was Robert E. Lee.

I also see this power to influence play out every day when clients refer their colleagues to us for participation in Rainmaker U. I instinctively know which leads are legitimate and worth following up on right away based upon the person making the referral.

For example, if my client Chris Rising refers someone to us, I'm quick to follow up. Chris has a very credible personal brand. A lot of people respect Chris and trust his judgment. In other words, "If Chris says Rainmaker U. is a first-rate program, it must be so."

How influential we are with our peers is a good way to gauge our personal brand credibility. Start paying attention to how often others take action because you did, or followed through because it was you who made the recommendation.

Another key indicator of how influential your personal brand is, is when others seek out your advice on issues beyond your area of expertise. What this means to me is that these people value you for more than just your knowledge. They also have great faith in your judgment and instincts.

THE ABILITY TO DRIVE POSITIVE CHANGE

Powerful personal brands can drive positive change. Nelson Mandela's personal brand played a major role in bringing down the walls of apartheid in South Africa. It may have taken 50 years, but we all know

Mandela is a patient man. In 1962, he was arrested and imprisoned on trumped-up political charges. He spent the next 27 years behind bars. A true man of principle, all Mandela had to do to be released by the white British government was admit to the charges levied against him. Mandela refused.

In 1990, the British government realized Mandela would never break. His symbolism of defiance was becoming more of a liability than his freedom would be. Mandela was finally released from prison on February 11, 1990. The wheels of change, championed by this charismatic hero, immediately began to pick up momentum. Four years after Mandela's release from prison, apartheid officially collapsed. One month later, Mandela was elected president of the country.

Today, Nelson Mandela may not hold political office (he retired from the presidency in 1999), but he is still a titanic figure on the world stage. When Nelson Mandela speaks, people listen.

Senator John McCain of Arizona is another person who can drive change because of the power of his personal brand. Senator McCain's personal brand is unmistakable: He is a *straight talker*. During his campaign for the Republican nomination for president in the 2000 election, McCain highlighted his personal brand by dubbing his traveling caravan the "Straight Talk Express."

Senator McCain is no one's lackey. He says what he thinks on any subject he wants, any time he wants, without fear of reprisal from his party. In a sense, McCain's personal brand transcends the Republican Party. Just as Katie Couric's personal brand is bigger than NBC, so too is John McCain's bigger than the Republican Party.[2]

---

2. So why might Senator John McCain not get elected president in 2008 if he is so beloved by the American people? Because before you make it to the general election, you must win your party's nomination. The Republican Party base is very conservative. Senator McCain's personal brand is more moderate than many in the base like. While Senator McCain's approval numbers exceed 50 percent with the public at large, his personal brand approval ratings with the Republican Party's rank-in-file is in the teens. Some polls even have him in the single digits. If Senator McCain cannot re-brand himself as more conservative, I suspect he will have a very difficult time earning his party's nomination.

McCain is sensitive to his stature and he uses his personal brand very strategically. In 2002 he used his clout to join forces with Democratic Senator Russ Feingold to push through campaign-finance reform. McCain was nonplussed by the fact that his biggest challengers in reforming the law were his fellow Republican senators, specifically the very powerful and conservative senator from Kentucky, Mitch McConnell. Not only did McCain successfully emerge from this ugly battle with new legislation, but he also added to his already vast reservoir of personal brand equity because of his willingness to put party politics aside and do what he believed was right.

The great personal brands in history were all titanic figures who changed the world:

- Lech Walesa was instrumental in bringing down the Iron Curtain.
- Rosa Parks helped ignite the Civil Rights Movement.
- Women vote today largely because of the personal brand of Susan B. Anthony.
- Lucille Ball paved the way for Carol Burnett, Roseanne Barr and Julia Louis-Dreyfus.

To be sure, each of the above individuals had talent and smarts. But so did many of their contemporaries. What made each of these icons so special was their personal brand. They all stood for something simple and identifiable, a quality that touched their audience's hearts in a way their contemporaries could not:

- Nelson Mandela—Honor
- Lech Walesa—Freedom
- Rosa Parks—Equality
- Susan B. Anthony—Self-determination
- Lucille Ball—Independence

The payoff for these titans has been so much more than fame and fortune; it is *immortality.* Time will pass, but our memories of these special personal brands never will.

I am not suggesting that in order to drive change everyone needs to be a titanic figure on the national or world stage with a huge personal brand like Katie Couric, Nelson Mandela or John McCain. I've discussed these three individuals merely to illustrate my point. If we are dedicated enough to do the work, we can certainly achieve our own levels of celebrity status with our targeted audiences.

Perhaps you are a top-flight attorney who wants to develop a personal brand that is synonymous with a particular practice area. For a period in my legal career, I worked with a plaintiff lawyer, Tom Girardi, who has become known as *The Lawyer in the Area of Toxic Torts.* When someone within the legal profession is looking for *The Toxic Tort Lawyer,* Tom Girardi's name is always at the top of the list.

The power of Tom Girardi's personal brand is undeniable. Tom's mere presence in a case instantly influences the dynamics of that case on many levels—from how the case is defended, to how it is handled by the lawyers on the other side, to the economic deal he is able to negotiate with the referring attorneys who sent him the case.

Tom's big payday that put him on the national toxic tort map came in 1996 when he won an arbitration award of nearly $400 million against Pacific Gas and Electric (PG&E) for negligent discharge of toxic substances into the water supply system of the town of Hinkley, located in California's Mojave Desert. The movie *Erin Brockovich,* starring Julia Roberts, was based on this case.

Girardi's victory changed the way the public viewed toxic tort cases. People began to realize they had rights against the big corporations doing business in their hometowns. The government also changed environmental regulations, and corporations soon modified the way they do business. For example, in 2005, GE's new president/CEO, Jeffrey Immelt, voluntarily agreed to pay as much as $100 million to clean up toxic discharge into the Hudson River by GE.

Up until Girardi prevailed against PG&E, toxic tort litigation was a very risky business for most lawyers with few players because, if a lawyer won his case, it could mean a multimillion-dollar payday, but if he lost, the costs incurred in financing a toxic tort case would almost certainly bankrupt his practice. You may recall another Hollywood movie, *A Civil Action,* starring John Travolta. In this film, the plaintiff's lawyer's career was all but destroyed because he bet on, and lost, a huge toxic tort case against W.R. Grace and Beatrice Foods.

Girardi's victory against PG&E cannot alone claim all the credit for making the toxic tort practice what it is today. However, he certainly had a lot to do with setting the wheels of change in motion.

Here are some other influential personal brands who have made the world a better place even though they are not household names:

- Mitch Snyder was an advocate for the homeless in the 80s who significantly helped change the way the country looked at and cared for the homeless. Snyder's personal brand was so influential because he walked the talk. For example, instead of living in a home in the suburbs of Washington, D.C., Snyder chose to live right alongside his constituency in a homeless shelter he helped build in one of D.C.'s roughest neighborhoods.

- Dorothy Courtney is the wife of a prominent attorney in Manhattan Beach, California. Many years back, one of her friends asked her to help out at a struggling shelter for battered women called Richstone Family Center. Because the Courtney name is well known and respected in Los Angeles, Dorothy was able to use her influence to raise millions of dollars for Richstone Family Center. Dorothy soon found herself running the shelter. Under her 20 years as Executive Director, the organization has grown from a

---

*Dorothy Courtney's husband is Bob Courtney, a very well-respected criminal defense lawyer in Southern California.

single community to an agency serving over 9,000 participants. It is safe to say not only did Dorothy Courtney
change Los Angeles' understanding of the problems of battered women, but also the lives of thousands of women
and children.

- Benjamin T. Rome is one of the largest donors to the
Catholic University of America, the pontifical university
of the U.S. What makes Benjamin so unique is he is
Jewish. Because of Benjamin's credibility in the Jewish
community, he was able to raise millions of Jewish dollars
for this Catholic institution.

- Do you know who Jim Murray was? From 1974 to 1983,
he was the general manager of the professional football
team the Philadelphia Eagles. He also started the Ronald
McDonald House. One of his players came to Jim in tears
because his son was dying of cancer. Murray pledged every
bit of his personal brand influence to help his player's son
win his fight. Murray's passion morphed into the Ronald
McDonald House.

I could go on for days with examples of people just like you and
me who had a passion to drive change and decided to use their personal brand appeal to make that change a reality. Here's my challenge
to you: Work to create *one* change in your community before you die
that makes your community a better place and continues on beyond
your years on Earth.

CAREER SECURITY AND STABILITY

A great personal brand also provides us with career security and stability in even the most uncertain of business environments. The days of
lifetime employment and guaranteed pensions are over. Today, not

only are we expected to perform at the highest level, but, even more important, we must be well liked if we are to rise to the top of our company or industry.

I recently read in *The Week* that, according to a Harvard Business School study, "A person's likeability is more important than his skills when it comes to getting hired or promoted, despite managers' claims to the contrary."

Having a great personal brand enhances our professional security and stability because it offers us options. The great personal brands always seem to have a knack for finding themselves at the doorstep of opportunity. To play on the old army recruiting slogan, "Companies are always looking for a few good personal brands." If our company goes out of business or our position becomes obsolete, having a great personal brand means we are not relegated to accepting whatever job offer we can find.

Because of Rainmaker U.'s vast network, it is not uncommon for one of our clients to ask us for help finding a better job. We can always quickly gauge what kind of work we have ahead of us based upon the attractiveness of the client's personal brand. One client we are helping right now will probably have several opportunities to choose from. Some of these will no doubt include fields where he has no experience. Why? Because in addition to having a proven track record, this client also presents his personal brand very well. Company leaders know it is much harder to teach an employee how to create and promote a great personal brand than it is to do the work (e.g., sell insurance, practice law or underwrite a loan).

Talent matters less than perception does. As I've said before and will repeat throughout this book, a great personal brand and average talent beats great talent and an average personal brand every time. The ability to do the work is a given. A personal brand is what makes us unique.

There are tens of thousands of excellent trial lawyers across the country, but there was only one Johnnie Cochran. There are thousands of talented CEOs, but only one Jack Welch. It takes some talent to get you into the game, but it takes a great personal brand to catapult you to celebrity status.

Ben Affleck's career is a case in point. Ben exploded onto the national stage in 1997 when he starred in the edgy independent film *Chasing Amy*. He followed up *Chasing Amy* with *Good Will Hunting*, for which he won an Oscar for best screenwriter. Affleck was soon thereafter coroneted by Hollywood as the next Rudolph Valentino. He quickly started commanding $15 million per picture.

Fast-forward six years. Ben Affleck's track record for blockbusters hasn't exactly been stellar. *Reindeer Games, Daredevil, Forces of Nature, Bounce, Daddy and Them, Surviving Christmas* and let's not forget that masterpiece of masterpieces *Gigli*. You remember these films, don't you? Me neither. So why does Ben Affleck still command top dollar? Because he has a bankable name. Hollywood's attitude is: Don't worry about the *talent thing,* your name will draw them in.

John F. Kennedy is another case where a great personal brand compensated for a modest track record. At the time of his assassination, Kennedy's presidency was in trouble. His reelection was anything but certain. In fact, President Kennedy's trip to Dallas was for purposes of showing his support in Texas, a state he had to win if he hoped to be reelected in 1964.

Kennedy had presided over the Bay of Pigs fiasco, the failed prevention of Israel's nuclear weapons program and the failed prevention of China's nuclear weapons program, yet decades later he is hailed as one of America's greatest presidents. Why? Because his political strategists carefully crafted the Camelot brand and then stealthily promoted that personal brand through the strategic circulation of photographs, writing of books, endless tributes and celebrations of Kennedy's life for more than four decades after his death. The result has been that we see the Kennedy presidency not necessarily for what it was, but for what his personal brand managers want us to see.

I know of one professional (we'll call him Bill) in the telecommunications industry who started out with such promise, but eventually fizzled out because he refused to work on and sell his personal brand.

Bill began his career with the granddaddy of all telecommunication companies, AT&T. At the time, AT&T was still a monopoly. Bill had an advantage because he started at the bottom flipping burgers in the company cafeteria, so there was only one direction to go. Early on, he moved up quickly. He was bright, handsome and very friendly. Those above him actually sought him out for promotion. His attraction was due to his personal brand appeal. His peers perceived him as *sharp*.

Once he hit management level, however, progress began to slow as the competition thickened. Bill was no longer the smartest or most capable of his peers. Distinction was not automatic. If he was to continue progressing, Bill would have to work at it. Bill had two options: He could choose to work his personal brand appeal and compete for promotions or he could lie down in the face of competition. Sadly, he chose the latter route.

Of course, Bill rationalizes his decision using all the typical platitudes: "I'm getting screwed because I don't play the game," "The only reason Tom got the promotion and I didn't was because Tom kissed the boss's butt," or my favorite, "My family's too important to me to work late or on weekends." His statements are merely noise masking the truth: (1) He didn't have the desire to compete for new opportunities and (2) he thinks he is smarter than everyone else and he wants them to come to him as opposed to him working his way into the inner circle.

Once it was apparent that this was the course he chose, Bill's fate was sealed. His wardrobe, which was once immaculate and stylish, is now drab. In the 25-plus years he's been at AT&T, he has not developed a single meaningful relationship with another business colleague, let alone any strategic alliances. Where in the past he was thought of by his colleagues as an enthusiastic go-getter, I am fairly certain that now no one thinks of Bill much at all.

The impact of Bill's choice has been devastating on his career. He is regularly passed over for promotions. For the last 10 years, AT&T has undergone metamorphosis after metamorphosis in an attempt to regain its once-prominent status as the leader of the industry. These metamorphoses have produced massive layoffs and reorganizations, and every time one of these events occur, Bill fights for his life in order to just hang on because he has nowhere else to go. His personal brand does not afford him the luxury of mobility.

My sister Mary Ellen and I always kid around that if each of the companies that either of us were working for were to go out of business, the last two people to leave would be us and the owner. From day one, we would practice the smart strategy. Build a personal brand that was so likeable, the boss couldn't bring himself to let us go, no matter the circumstances. The only thing that would put us out of a job was the company actually going out of business.

I'm always amused when I see the talent and knowledge purists throwing temper tantrums when their accomplishments are overshadowed by others who may not be as talented but who have a much better personal brand. Danica Patrick is one of my favorite examples.

Danica Patrick is arguably one of the reigning superstars in the Indy Racing League despite never having actually won a race in open-wheel competition. Her male counterparts are apoplectic over the public's adulation. One competitor, Dan Wheldon, who won the 2005 Indy 500, in which Danica came in fourth, went so far as to have T-shirts made up with the phrase, "I actually won the Indy 500." The net result of his message: "I am bitter that I was the one who actually won the race and yet no one is paying any attention to me. Danica hasn't won a thing and she's getting all the attention. This is unfair." Not tough to figure out this guy's personal brand. *Cry Baby? Sour Puss? Poor Sport?*

Following the Indy 500, things got worse for Danica. Jealous of her long autograph lines, many of Danica's fellow drivers gave her the cold shoulder. What these catty competitors refuse to accept is that great talent alone is no match for a great personal brand.

As I watched this controversy unfold, I couldn't help but wonder to myself, *Do you think these guys would have felt differently if they had been in Danica's shoes?* Would they have said, "No, don't pay attention to me. I don't deserve it. Focus on my colleagues." I don't think so. Instead of whining about how unfair things are, they should focus on how to make their personal brands as attractive as Danica's.

In the late 90s, the same phenomenon swept through the world of women's tennis in the personhood of Anna Kournikova. Women's tennis had never seen anything like her. Blonde, young and beautiful. Anna was like the reincarnation of Chrissie Evert times 20. She was Marilyn Monroe with a racquet. The media loved her, the public couldn't get enough of her and her fellow competitors hated her because she hogged the spotlight.

By the time Anna retired from tennis at the ripe old age of 22, she had won a grand total of zero singles matches. Not one. Yet her earnings from her personal brand endorsements dwarfed the winnings of all of her competitors combined.

Anna's detractors, like Danica's, complained endlessly about how bad Anna Kournikova was for their sport. They whined that Anna's personal brand was shifting the public's attention away from what they perceived to be most important—the talent of the other women tennis players. What these complainers refused to come to grips with was that the public didn't care about their talent. All they wanted was more of Anna.

What they also conveniently overlooked was how Anna's *sexy* personal brand enhanced all of their careers and bank accounts. Wherever Anna played, crowds followed. The large crowds drove up advertising rates that translated into more lucrative tournament purses and endorsement deals. If the whiners had been smart, they would have spent their off hours joining the rest of the tennis world in their chant of "We want Anna!"

I am not saying that the Danica and Anna phenomenons are fair or right. All I am pointing out is reality. It is a waste of time trying to change what the public wants. We can't. Our objective is to find out what makes our target audience feel good and then give it to them in the form of our personal brand.

THE POWER OF PULL

Every day millions of us wake up and go to work at the proverbial salt mine—*pushing and pushing and pushing,* all in an effort to move the stone just a fraction of an inch forward. And there always seems to be someone determined to block our progress. Maybe it's the reception-ist/gatekeeper who denies us access to our prospects, voicemail and caller-ID that allow others to screen our calls or our inability to differ-entiate ourselves from others in the crowded marketplace. At the end of the day, we feel tired and worn down—like Sisyphus pushing the boulder up the hill, only to have it roll back down over us. And because we have no other options, we wake up and engage in this same routine, day after day after day.

In sharp contrast, the great personal brands enjoy the power of *pull.* *Pull* is when your reputation precedes you to the point that oth-ers seek you out and pull you forward. Opportunity finds you, rather than you *pushing* to find it. When this dynamic happens, these great personal brands enjoy the greatest of all payoffs—*true freedom*—the ability to do what they want, when they want, with whomever they want. We know we've achieved true freedom when (1) we can name our price, (2) we can pass on clients we don't like and (3) a steady stream of people are calling to ask us to help them.

Zig Ziglar is an icon in my business. The other day I read that Zig Ziglar has not marketed for new business in over 25 years. You literal-ly have to book him 18 months in advance. Now that's pull!

Zig is also a very modest man. He willingly admits that things have not always been this way. Like most successful people, Zig traveled for many years, plying his wares in a lot of nowhere towns, speaking to a lot of nobodies before his message finally caught on. His big break came when Mary Kay Ash of Mary Kay Cosmetics saw him speak. At the invitation of Ms. Ash, Zig began traveling all over America to speak to Mary Kay reps.

Today, Zig Ziglar commands top dollar, a pricy $25,000 per engagement. On one of his audiobook series, Zig recounts a conversation he had with a woman who couldn't believe he was paid as much as he was for a single presentation. The conversation went something like this:

"Mr. Ziglar, you are good but $25,000 is a lot of money for an hour presentation."

Zig, ever the gentleman, responded, "Madame, I'm not paid $25,000 for one hour. I'm paid $25,000 for all the thousands of hours I spent perfecting my craft and researching the gems I shared with you today that can change your life in an instant."

CHAPTER SUMMARY

Key Points

The payoff for having a great personal brand:
- Fame and fortune
- The power to influence
- The ability to drive positive change
- Career security and stability
- The power of pull

FIVE

Differentiate Yourself or Die

Manufacturing no longer drives the American economy; service providers do. According to the Department of Labor, in 2005 the service industry accounted for 79.2 percent of the total GDP. Products we can touch and feel no longer dominate the landscape of commercial transactions. People and their personal brands do.

To paraphrase Harry Beckwith, author of the bestseller *Selling the Invisible,* the majority of Americans today make their living selling something that is just that—invisible.

The bulk of commercial business in America centers on three disciplines: professional services (such as lawyers, accountants and financial service providers), technology specialists and sales and marketing experts. While it is true that Dell and Nike are shipping low-paying manufacturing jobs overseas, there has been an explosion of new white-collar service sector jobs in America. Siemens, the Europe-based financial conglomerate, poured more than 60,000 new white-collar service sector jobs into the U.S. in 2004. In 2005, 8–10 million Americans were working in purely service sector jobs, up from 3–4 million in 2003. The trend is irreversible. Those who refuse to embrace it will be left behind.

There are three reasons this shift away from a product-driven economy to a service-driven economy makes personal branding more important than ever: (1) the customer's buying strategy, (2) fierce competition and (3) information overload.

THE CUSTOMER'S BUYING STRATEGY

If we are not selling a product, we are selling something that is invisible. For example, customers cannot see and touch litigation results, financial service strategies or insurance coverage. The challenge, however, for the professional service provider is that even though the marketplace has shifted from the sale of products to the sale of services, the customer's purchasing strategy remains the same. Eighty percent of all buyers are visual. This means buyers still need to *see something* in order to help them validate their purchasing decisions. *Something* must replace the tangible product. That *something* is our personal brand. Like it or not, most of the time success boils down to little more than a popularity contest. He who has the most likeable personal brand wins.

I am confronted with this reality every day in my own business. As I mentioned in previous chapters, our core business at The Personal Branding Group centers on our Rainmaker U. program. People who go through Rainmaker U. often refer their friends and colleagues to us. When this happens, the process is typically the same: Someone from our team talks to the prospect on the phone and explains our program in detail. If the prospect expresses interest, we invite him to peruse our website for more information. Two to three days later, we follow up to see if the prospect is interested in joining the program.

If a candidate is genuinely interested, by the time we follow up, in addition to reviewing our website he will have also probably consulted with others who have been through the program. Even after all this due diligence, and even though he may be 100 percent convinced of the program's value, it is not unusual for a candidate to still hold off on committing. Something still holds him back. The candidate may not even know what it is, but I do.

In order for the individual to be comfortable making a commitment, he needs to *see something* to which he can become emotionally attached. That *something* is very often me. And when it comes to me, how good I am is not nearly as important as the perception of how good I may be. The question these candidates are looking to answer is, "Is this guy worth a $6,000 investment?"

Make no mistake—quality is not nearly as important as the perception of quality. Just take note of the Coca-Cola versus Pepsi advertising wars. Coca-Cola is by far the most valuable brand in the world. It is estimated to be worth $5 billion. Coca-Cola easily outsells Pepsi every single year. Yet, year after year, Pepsi outperforms Coca-Cola in taste tests. The message here is very straightforward: It doesn't matter who *is* really the best; what matters is who the people perceive to be the best.

Perception is just as relevant when it comes to personal branding. Did you know that most people think tall people are smarter than short people?[1]

In his bestselling book *The Tipping Point*, Malcolm Gladwell references a study conducted by a group of social scientists that seems to validate this hypothesis. These social scientists positioned two boys, one taller than the other, playing ball in a schoolyard. They also invited 100 adults to attend a function at the same school at the same time the boys were playing ball. As part of the experiment, the facilitators made it impossible for the invitees to find the entrance to the school unless they asked the boys for help. More than 90 percent of the invitees went straight to the taller boy for directions.

According to John Adams, George Washington was unanimously selected to lead the Continental Army because "he was the tallest man in the room" and "he had a majestic deportment."

---

1. At 5' 7 1/2" on a good day, I would certainly quarrel with this hypothesis.

How about this one? I recently read of a study done by Princeton University researchers that found that politicians with craggy, masculine features are 70 percent more likely to be elected to public office than those with rounded, cherubic features.

Want more? A study done by social scientists at North Carolina State University found that average-looking people out-earn below-average-looking people by 10 percent and above-average-looking people command, on average, 19 percent more in pay than below-average-looking people.

Are all of these statistics a reflection of what's true (e.g., that tall is smarter than short)? Probably not, but truth is often irrelevant. What is relevant is the buyer's perception. Therefore, we must waste no more time. We have to start managing our buyers' perceptions by crystallizing and intentionally promoting our personal brand. Otherwise, we may find ourselves scrambling for survival.

Many times I have consulted with professional service firms on the subject of business development, only to find that they had spent tens of thousands of dollars building their entire marketing strategy around technical competence, educational pedigree and customer service. Unfortunately, it is my job to break the bad news to these firms that they have wasted a lot of time and money promoting nothing particularly special. Top-notch performance, intelligence and service are a prerequisite to even competing for the business.

In my work with professionals, executives and politicians, it does not matter how smart or good they are at their craft. What is important is what they believe are their most likeable qualities. Business development and career success are built upon what I call "hand-to-hand contact": pressing the flesh, building rapport, going deep with people. If buyers like our personal brand, not only are they going to choose us over the competition, chances are they'll even pay more for what we have to offer.

FIERCE COMPETITION

The fierce competition between professionals in today's marketplace is the second reason having an effective personal brand is essential. Almost everything each of us does for a living has been commoditized. The financial services industry is a case in point.

It used to be that if we wanted a loan we went to a bank, if we needed insurance we called an insurance agent and if we wanted to buy and sell equities we consulted our stockbroker. This has all changed.

With the passage of Gramm-Leach-Bliley in 1999, financial services have become a virtual free-for-all. An insurance agent in Southern California suddenly finds himself competing with thousands of stockbrokers who now call themselves "financial planners" as well as with thousands of bank officers who also fancy themselves "financial specialists." The points of differentiation in the financial services industry are becoming fewer and fewer.

I read a startling statistic in Thomas L. Friedman's *New York Times* bestseller, *The World Is Flat.* In 2003, the tax returns for 25,000 United States citizens were prepared by workers in India. In 2004, this figure rose to 100,000. In 2005, it was 500,000. Friedman went on to say, "In the future, anything that can be devalued and digitized will be done in India or elsewhere."

Have you heard how Los Angeles–based residential homebuilder behemoth KB Homes is fighting commoditization? They have recently unveiled the first of a series of Martha Stewart home communities. These homes are priced between $200,000 and $400,000 and will be designed by the diva herself. The first community will be located in Cary, North Carolina, a suburb of Raleigh. Sound silly? Well, more than 3,800 families have already expressed interest in the first 650-home community.

The lesson we must quickly learn if we hope to thrive in today's competitive business environment is: No matter how good our skills, resources and knowledge are, the competition's are just as good. Does anybody really think Skadden Arps has better trial lawyers than Cravath,

Swaine & Moore or that Northwestern Mutual has better life insurance programs than New York Life? I assure you that the accountants at Pricewaterhouse are just as smart as their counterparts at KPMG and Ernst & Young. Building a great personal brand is the most powerful and definitive separator we have because no matter what happens with the economy, our industry or society, there is only one of each of us.

I suggest that the reason my client Curtis Estes is routinely in the top 20 agents out of 7,000 at Northwestern Mutual Financial Network (NMFN) is not because of Northwestern's products and services. It is because Curtis' personal brand sells better than his competition's. The same is true for my client Anthony Marguleas, who is one of the top residential real estate brokers in Los Angeles and owner of Amalfi Estates, a boutique firm catering to buyers of exclusive homes in California's Pacific Palisades. This year Anthony is on track to do $100 million in sales.[2]

The same can be said of my client Mindy Day-Hodges, who was recently nominated for the Los Angeles Women Making a Difference award.

I am fairly certain that, somewhere out there, there are probably better salespeople than Curtis, better residential real estate agents than Anthony and better money managers than Mindy, but that doesn't matter because being the best is not their differentiation factor—their personal brand is.

INFORMATION OVERLOAD

Information overload is the third reason building a compelling personal brand is a must. The average person will be bombarded by more than 1,000 electronic messages this week alone. Most young adults will have watched well over 1 million commercials by the time they are 18

---

2. Anthony actually earned more than $400,000 in commissions in the month of May alone.

years old. Every day, 4,000 new books are published. As the availability of time shrinks and information explodes, the importance of personal branding increases.

Amidst all this noise, our personal brand plays an invaluable role in simplifying the complexity of our buyers' choices. An effective personal brand is a safe haven in a world of information chaos. The personal brands that win today are those that filter out this noise. The best personal brands offer something specific and simple. They present themselves as the safe choice.

Beckwith summed it up perfectly in *What Clients Love:* "The people who win today are the filterers, simplifiers, and clarifiers." People crave clarity. Beckwith was also right when he said, "The ability to deliver a single simple point is a lost art."

I see some of my friends in the insurance industry struggling to find their footing amidst the blizzard of changes and consolidation going on within the financial services industries. NMFN is a case in point. For over 100 years, they have set the standard for excellence when it comes to life insurance. Seeing the writing on the wall within the industry, NMFN has begun an internal campaign, pushing their agents to promote themselves as comprehensive financial services advisors.

To assist its agents in branding themselves, NMFN: (1) has changed its name from Northwestern Mutual Life Insurance to Northwestern Mutual Financial Network and (2) in 1998–1999 acquired and added the Frank Russell Company to its platform of services.

I think the name change and enlarged platform are actually hindrances to their agents. Northwestern has done such a good job branding itself as an insurance company that clients and prospects become confused when agents start talking about investment securities. What Northwestern has really done is complicate the choice for the buyer.

Can NMFN's agents overcome the disadvantage? Only time will tell. NMFN's agents will only succeed if they can synthesize all of their disparate parts into one unified, unambiguous message.

I wonder if NMFN would better serve its insurance agents by opening a financial services company under a different name with a different cadre of agents.

Contrast NMFN's agents with my client Joey Behrstock, who is also an insurance agent. Joey is with Gilbert-Krupin of Beverly Hills. When Joey introduces himself at a networking function, his message is plain and unequivocal. "I do one thing: I sell life insurance." It doesn't get any simpler than that.

Let me give you firsthand proof of the effectiveness of Joey's strategy. Joey and an agent from another leading insurance company were in the same Rainmaker U. class. In these classes, we frequently group students in threes for purposes of exchanging ideas and working through exercises. During these groupings, the participants have a chance to do some networking as well as explain to one another in more detail what they do for a living. On one occasion, Joey found himself paired up with the insurance agent from the other company as well as with a private equity investor. The three worked together for 30 minutes and at the conclusion of the exercise the private equity investor turned to Joey and asked him right in front of the other agent, "I need to get five million in life insurance. Can you help me?"

When Joey relayed this story to me, he also confided that he was somewhat embarrassed by the awkwardness of the moment; the other agent stood by silently, I'm sure just a little surprised by his apparent invisibility. A few weeks later, I did some due diligence of my own. I called the private equity investor and asked him about what happened. Specifically, I wanted to know why he asked Joey for insurance instead of the other guy. His response was simple and straightforward, "I knew Joey sold insurance. I had no clue what the other guy did."

My experience has been that the personal brand that stands for a single, powerful message wins every time. In this day of information overload, four words sum it up perfectly: "Simple good, complex bad."

CHAPTER SUMMARY

Key Points

■ America's service-driven economy makes personal branding more important than ever.

■ When we sell a service, we are selling something invisible. Bear in mind, 80 percent of all buyers are visual, which means they still need to *see something* to validate their decision. That *something* is us.

■ Commoditization makes differentiation harder and harder. The only thing that remains unique is *us*.

■ People are drowning in information. They don't want more, they want less. The people who win today are the simplifiers, filterers and synthesizers.

SIX

A Lasting Competitive Advantage

More than just giving us a powerful emotional connection with our audience, a great personal brand also guarantees us two distinct advantages over our competition: (1) more focus and (2) a powerful reserve of goodwill for the times when we misstep.

FOCUS

Believe it or not, most people will never take the time to crystallize their personal brand, let alone lay out a strategy to promote that brand. This is great news for the rest of us who are focused on working, day in and day out, on our personal brand.

Perhaps you have heard this statistic: 80 percent of all sales are made after the fifth contact. Of the 100 percent who make that first contact, 40 percent make the third, 25 percent the fourth, and 10 percent the fifth. The same principle applies to personal branding: A lot of people want a great personal brand, but very few do what it takes to build one.

A personal brand is an extremely effective focusing tool because it centralizes all of our business development and career advancement activities. Having the proper focus can be extraordinarily powerful. For example, diffused light merely illuminates; when focused, however, light can be so much more. Manipulated by a magnifying glass, that same light can set grass and paper on fire. Focused even more, it becomes a laser beam capable of penetrating steel.

A great personal brand can do the same for us. Our personal brand should influence just about everything we do: how we dress, communicate what we do, entertain, network, and so on. If we are passionate about our personal brand, the intensity of our focus and the intentionality of our actions will propel us to levels we never imagined. The challenge for most people is that they never get passionate about aligning their day-to-day behaviors and activities with the values and qualities for which they want to stand. If we invest the time and effort, we will see how our consistent execution of the small things dramatically enhances our personal brand credibility.

My friend Patrick McNicholas, a plaintiff personal injury lawyer with the law firm McNicholas and McNicholas, is an amazingly likeable guy. Colleagues, judges, juries, everybody loves Pat—and it is this likeability that has made him one of the most successful trial lawyers in Southern California.

I know firsthand that Pat labors long and hard in protecting and promoting his personal brand. He is an impeccable dresser during trial, a gentleman to the court staff, respectful to judges and gracious to opposing counsel. Pat is also well prepared and extremely professional when presenting his case.

Pat will also be the first to tell you, though smart he is, his legal scholarship is not what usually wins his cases. As a matter of fact, getting tangled up in legal minutia of a case is not Pat's favorite part of practicing law; but when it comes to capitalizing on his likeability factor in front of a jury, few rival him.

In May 2005, Pat tried a personal injury case in Compton, California. His adversary was a formidable defense attorney who has a reputation for pulling rabbits out of hats.

As is the practice with jury trials, after each side had had its chance to present its own evidence, each lawyer was asked to give a summation of the key points of his case to the jury in a final attempt to persuade the jury to enter a verdict in favor of his client. The defense attorney went first and, as predicted, delivered a very effective summation on behalf of his client. Then it was Pat's turn.

At the conclusion of his summation, Pat made a request to the jurors to award his client a specific dollar amount in damages. When making such a request, an attorney will typically inflate the amount of damages. The request is understood by the attorneys to be a suggested ballpark figure. Neither side ever expects the jury to award exactly what is requested.

In this case, Pat explained to the jury, "Ladies and gentlemen, if you award anything less than $10 million to my client, the defense will consider it a victory for their side." After deliberating for several hours, the jury returned a verdict in favor of Pat's client for $10,030,000. The fact that the jury awarded Pat's client exactly what Pat asked for is a testament to his likeable personal brand.

Clients hire Pat because they instinctively know that if their case ever goes to trial, the jury will instantly trust him. They know this because that is exactly how *they* feel about him.

My own personal brand has also played a very influential role in just about every aspect of my decision-making process, including the small details of personal grooming. I remember two years ago, I was traveling from California to see my family in New Jersey. I booked my reservation on JetBlue for the Saturday 7:00 a.m. flight out of Long Beach, California.

I live in Los Angeles, so in order to make it to the airport on time, I had to be on the road by 4:30 a.m. Since I am not an early riser, I had no plans to shave or shower. A baseball cap, sweatshirt and sweatpants with sneakers would have to do.

When I arrived at JFK Airport in New York four and a half hours later, a driver was waiting for me. I hopped into the back of the Lincoln Town Car and directed the driver to take me to my parents' church, St. Joseph's, so I could make the 5:30 p.m. mass. Going to Saturday evening mass would allow me to maximize the time I could spend with my parents and the rest of my family on Sunday morning.

As I got closer to the church, I took a quick glance at myself in the car's rearview mirror to make some last-minute adjustments in my appearance. Having traveled eight hours, being ungroomed and sloppily dressed, it didn't take much for me to realize I looked like a bum. My appearance certainly did not represent my personal brand very well. While I could have attended church without much worry, I knew in my heart that how I looked was totally incongruent with how I wanted others to perceive me. So I asked the driver to take me directly to my parents' home. I would attend church the following day, looking like the gentleman I want to be seen as.

Though this is a small story, its message is by no means insignificant. Great personal brands are built through alignment and congruency of the personal brand and the person's day-to-day behaviors and activities. For our personal brand to have influence, we must live it day in and day out in everything we do and say—particularly when it comes to the little stuff. Anybody can manage the obvious. The truly special personal brand separates itself from the pack by paying attention to the little details that most others either overlook or don't care to pay attention to.

Another of my corporate clients, Buchanan Street Partners, offers a great example of intentional alignment of behavior with its team members' personal brands. Buchanan Street contends in a very competitive marketplace, providing commercial real estate financing to developers across the country. Early on in the establishment of their company, Buchanan Street's executive team knew that if they were going to be successful in what is largely a commodity business, they would have to find a way to differentiate themselves from their competitors.

Below is a sampling of the steps they have taken to make sure everyone is properly focused at all times:

- After several of their people went through our Rainmaker U. program, Buchanan's execs decided that the company would be recognized as having the best-dressed people in the business. I can't tell you how many times I've heard others say, "I can always tell a Buchanan Street guy because of the way he's dressed."

- Buchanan's president, Robert Brunswick, has made it a requirement that every person in the firm be crystal clear about what his personal brand is and that everyone else be aware of everyone else's brand too. The purpose of this is so that the team can hold one another accountable.

- Robert and the executive team have a similar requirement for everyone's personal vision statement. At last count, Robert had had 72 personal vision statements emailed to him for approval by January 1, 2005.

- Every producer in the company is also required to memorize the company's 15-Second Commercial (aka "the elevator pitch") so that when someone asks anyone in the company, "What do you do for a living?" that person will dazzle his audience with a concise, articulate value statement.

- Buchanan Street also has drafted company Standards for Success (aka "The Buchanan Code of Excellence"), which are posted prominently in the office and to which everyone is expected to adhere.

- Buchanan requires every member of the team to complete two personal development/educational programs per year so that everyone continues to grow as people, not just producers.

These six simple yet impactful examples demonstrate how a company understands and embraces the belief that the credibility of the company's overall message in the marketplace is only as strong as the commitment of each individual team member to live in alignment with that message.

You might have noticed that the six examples I chose to highlight have little or nothing to do with the production of business. Buchanan subscribes to the principle, "Let's get the people right and the business will take care of itself."

Buchanan's success is fueled in part by the marketing mediocrity of its competition. A common refrain I hear from others in Buchanan's industry is, "Just get me in the *right* room with the *right* people and I'll close 'em." I've seen much of Buchanan's competition and it's precisely this way of thinking that causes them to continue to lose market share.

Whenever people say to me, "Just get me in a room . . . ," I can't help but wonder if these people realize that something must be wrong with the way they package and market themselves if they are always trying to find and force their way into this "magical," right room. Doesn't it make so much more sense for them to work on their personal brand until they became so irresistible that they are regularly invited into the networking circles of other superstars?

It has also been my experience that most people who follow the "Just get me in a room . . ." philosophy would do no better than they do now if they did, indeed, find themselves in a roomful of the "right" prospects.

Here's a list of some obvious things we should all make sure are in alignment with our personal brand:

- Our brochure (i.e., content and quality)
- Our website, including our bio
- Our office space
- The quality of delivery of our products/services
- Our dress, grooming and manners

- The way our receptionist answers our phones
- How we treat our staff
- How our team handles our clients
- The credibility of the company for which we work
- How we respond to difficulties

These examples are not only obvious, but are also the easiest areas in which to make changes because they usually involve very little personal risk. The greatest impact on our personal brand occurs when we have the courage to change more personal aspects of ourselves and our business, such as our habits, attitudes, friends we hang around with and so on.

Here's a helpful technique I use to focus myself to ensure that my behavior and actions are, as much as possible, in full alignment with my personal brand. As you will learn in Chapter Nine, the personal brand I have chosen to promote for myself is *expert*. When I am uncertain about what to do, I ask myself one simple question: "If I am *the expert* in my field, what should I do?" The answer always crystallizes swiftly and clearly. Then it is just a matter of commitment and implementation. I overlay this question to as many component parts of me and my business until I am satisfied I know with absolute certainty what I need to do in each category in order to reinforce my personal brand.

We encourage you to start paying attention to:

- Who your friends are—jettison people who undermine your credibility.
- Unprofessional drinking and drug habits—stop it.
- Following through on your word, especially when it is a huge inconvenience.
- Well-roundedness (current events and interests beyond your profession)—be interesting.
- Your 15-Second Commercial—sharp, crisp, compelling.
- Your Uniqueness Statement (yes, it is different from your 15-Second Commercial).

- Honesty—tell the truth, always, no matter how painful.
- Bragging—stop it. Don't tell people you are *great*. Just *be* great.
- Self-discipline—practice delay-gratification.
- Attitude—positive can-do.
- Treat everyone equally (don't just pay lip service to this principle. Strive to be Gandhi-like).
- Be a spectacular public speaker—work your butt off at it. It's a craft to be honed.

I could go on forever. These are just some of the categories I struggle to improve on daily. Look to consistently make small improvements every day. Don't equate slow progress with no progress. Lasting change takes time, especially when we are trying to change life-time habits.

Keep in mind that when the steward of an aircraft carrier wants to change the direction of the ship's travel, he must input new coordinates into the ship's steering instruments. That same aircraft carrier pro-grammed with the new directional coordinates will continue to travel an additional 20 miles in its original direction before it even begins registering any perceptible change.

And so it will be with many of us as we work to align our behaviors with our personal brand. Sometimes noticeable change can take a long time.

GOODWILL

Having a great personal brand also prepares us for those times when we make mistakes. *Everyone* makes mistakes, no matter how good they are. A person's ability to recover from his major mistakes depends upon two things: (1) how he responds to the crisis and (2) the amount of good-will he has built up and can draw upon.

Goodwill is measured by how willing people are to forgive us when we misstep. If others are willing to let our mistakes slide, we are probably fairly well liked. If others are not willing to let a blunder go, chances are we've misbehaved in the past.

I believe that most people in America are wired to forgive. It is part of our country's soul. America is the land of second (and sometimes third, fourth and fifth) chances. We just have to give our peers a reason to want to forgive us.

Let's compare two examples, Hugh Grant and Pete Rose. Both men were guilty of behavior that was totally inconsistent with their personal brand. When caught with a prostitute in Hollywood, California, Hugh Grant responded proactively and capitalized on a deep reservoir of goodwill he had built up playing lovable roles in such hit movies as *Four Weddings and a Funeral* and *Nine Months*. Pete Rose, on the other hand, adopted a bunker mentality when his gambling transgressions were exposed, squandering all of his goodwill. By the time he did eventually fess up, it was too late.

If you remember, shortly after Hugh Grant was arrested he appeared on *The Tonight Show* to apologize to his girlfriend and his fans, as well as to poke fun at himself. Through his apology he asked for our forgiveness, and because of the wellspring of goodwill he had built up over the years, the public willingly forgave him. Hugh Grant has never looked back.

Pete Rose handled his situation in exactly the opposite fashion. Rose's mantra from day one was "deny, deny, deny until the issue of gambling on baseball goes away." The problem for Pete was the evidence. It was so overwhelming that every time Pete denied the charges or attacked his accusers, he used up a portion of the goodwill he had built up over the years as *Charlie Hustle* and a member of the Cincinnati Reds' *Big Red Machine*. By the time Pete Rose owned up to gambling illegally on sports, including baseball, it was too late. He had no goodwill left in the tank. His pleas for forgiveness and statements of contrition have, for the most part, fallen on deaf ears.

There are two keys to redemption. First, redemption will absolutely, positively not happen unless before our fall from grace we have given people something to like about us. Second, we must genuinely ask for others' forgiveness.

The respective presidencies of Bill Clinton and Richard Nixon offer the perfect comparison. Both men lied to the American people. One was beloved by his constituency before he betrayed the people's trust; the other was not. One eventually owned up to the truth and asked for forgiveness. The other went to his grave stubbornly refusing to acknowledge the error of his ways. One left the office of the presidency hailed by many as a great president; the other resigned ignominiously.

It is amazing how far people will go to protect those they love and admire. Just ask the attorneys who practice plaintiff personal injury law in Southern California. These attorneys know that a personal injury case against Disneyland is usually worth only half of what it would be if it were against any other defendant. Why? Because jurors in Orange County, California, cannot bring themselves to believe that Mickey Mouse or Donald Duck would ever do anything to hurt kids and their families.

Did you know that, historically, physicians who are sued for medical malpractice prevail in seven out of ten trials? This is a staggeringly high success ratio. Why is this so? Because as a society we revere our doctors, and most juries have a difficult time believing that the same doctors that save our lives are also guilty of making terrible mistakes. Only in the most egregious instances are doctors found liable.

If we have built up enough goodwill, we should not be surprised at how forgiving our peers can be.

In January 2005, Richard Scrushy, the CEO of HealthSouth, went on trial for accounting fraud in the amount of $2.7 billion. The indictment against him, if proven, would have been the largest corporate fraud case against a CEO in U.S. history. By all accounts Scrushy was going down; the evidence of criminal wrongdoing was overwhelming. But the prosecution underestimated one very powerful factor: Scrushy was adored by Birmingham, Alabama, the community in which he was going to be tried.

Long before there was any suspicion of wrongdoing, Scrushy labored to build goodwill within the community. Just a sampling of Scrushy's good deeds for the people of Birmingham included donating $600,000 for church construction and $250,000 for the construction of a school, pledging millions of dollars for arthritis and cerebral palsy research, serving as Chair of Alabama's Sports Hall of Fame and serving on the Board of Trustees for two Alabama colleges.

When it came time to try Scrushy, not only was *he* going on trial, but Birmingham's favorite son as well. The trial lasted five months, more than 1 million pieces of evidence were introduced against Scrushy, and dozens of credible witnesses testified against him. So certain of victory, the prosecution spent a fortune on its case. To the surprise of those following the trial, and probably to the surprise of Richard Scrushy himself, he was acquitted on all counts.

The goodwill that Richard Scrushy had built up was too much for even the prosecution's slam-dunk case.*

Contrast that with the former CEO of Tyco, Dennis Kozlowski. Reading press clippings of Kozlowski's gluttony and arrogance, many people couldn't wait for him to go down. He was a 21st-century Caligula, using company money for such indulgences as a $7,000 shower curtain, throwing his wife an obscenely lavish birthday party and purchasing a $7 million apartment for himself and his mistresses.

To no one's surprise, Kozlowski was convicted and at the time of sentencing the judge threw the book at him, giving Kozlowski 25 years. And because of the way some of the charges against Kozlowski had been filed by the prosecution, he will spend a certain portion of his time in a maximum security prison as opposed to a Club Fed.

---

* Scrushy may have gotten off in Birmingham, but the federal government's prosecution in Montgomery, Alabama, was a different story. In June 2006, Scrushy was convicted of bribery and mail fraud in connection with campaign contributions to former Democratic Governor of Alabama, Dan Siegelman.

Hopefully, most of us will never be confronted with Scrushy- or Kozlowski-type circumstances. Our missteps will likely be more banal in comparison. Nonetheless, we are mistaken if we think any errors we could make will be so small that building an ample reservoir of good-will would be a waste of time. Rest assured, during our lifetimes, we will say or do something stupid that will offend someone important. Sometime, somewhere, we will be guilty of a lapse in judgment that is so inconsistent with who we are that people may question our integrity. It is in these moments that we will be well served by having a deep reservoir of goodwill to draw upon.

My dad once said to me, "Son, life insurance is the best money you hope to waste. You hope never to have to use it, but if you need it you're glad it's there." The same can be said of goodwill.

Having a vast reservoir of goodwill is useless unless we know how to access it. The only way to access goodwill is to genuinely and unconditionally ask our peers for forgiveness. If we are unable to apologize, we might as well forget any hope of being forgiven.

As forgiving as people are, they typically will not extend their forgiveness voluntarily. We must ask for it sincerely. In 1995, NFL great Warren Moon was charged with assaulting his wife, Felicia, in a domestic dispute. What made this incident particularly damaging to Moon's reputation was that he was universally recognized by fans, colleagues and the media as a superb human being, a first-class teammate and the quintessential community man.

Rather than hiding behind a wall of silence and hoping everything would blow over, Warren Moon, with Felicia by his side, held a press conference and apologized. He asked for all our support, understanding and prayers as he and his wife worked through their difficult times. Moon's apology was more than just words; he backed it up with deeds, attending counseling and openly speaking to the press and community about the wrongness of domestic abuse.

Moon's sincerity was real and the public quickly forgave him. There has never been even a hint of another such incident in his life.

His apology was sincere and his contrition real. In 2006, Warren Moon was elected to the NFL Hall of Fame. It couldn't have happened to a nicer guy.

In addition to being sincere, our request for forgiveness must be unconditional. During the Vietnam War, Jane Fonda engaged in what some would call treasonous behavior. Though she escaped criminal prosecution, she did not avoid the public's scorn. And for more than 30 years, Jane Fonda has been reviled by a good portion of the public, who commonly refer to her as "Hanoi Jane." To this day, any movie in which Jane Fonda appears is prohibited from being shown on any American military base anywhere in the world. For nearly 30 years, Jane Fonda had refused to apologize for her error in judgment.

In 2005, Fonda attempted to change the perception many Americans had of her by writing her memoirs. As part of her book tour, Fonda appeared on many television programs, including *60 Minutes.* Instead of coming out and unconditionally apologizing, saying, "What I did was foolish and misguided. I am sorry," Fonda finessed the issue. Her ego just couldn't allow her to admit she may have done something foolish and hurt a lot of people in the process. Rather, Fonda tried to spin the issue as if the public somehow misunderstood the passion and impulsiveness of a young activist.

Millions of dollars of media opportunity later, Jane Fonda still remains a pariah with much of the same audience she had hoped to win over through her book tour.

Here is my advice to you: When you make a mistake, own it! Admit your mistake right away and sincerely ask for forgiveness. You will rarely be disappointed by the response. Remember, "The coward dies a thousand times; the hero just once."

CHAPTER SUMMARY

Key Points

- Having a great personal brand gives us two distinct advantages over our competition:
    1. More focus
    2. A huge reservoir of goodwill for those times when we misstep

SEVEN

The Talent Question

I've made a big deal so far over my belief that talent is overrated. This does not mean, however, that we do not have to have talent to be a superstar in our industry. People who buy our personal brand do so because of the promises we make, either directly or indirectly, about our ability to deliver. There is no surer way to undermine our personal brand credibility than to fail to deliver on our promises. Therefore, we must have a certain amount of talent to perform at the level expected of us.

TALENT IS MORE THAN JUST NATURAL ABILITY

Natural ability is the starting point. The greatest personal brands in history recognized early on that they had special abilities and they worked very hard and intentionally to develop those abilities to their fullest potential. Natural ability will certainly get us started down the road to success, but if we do not develop our special talents, at some point we will plateau.

At the height of Michael Jordan's career, he had five personal coaches and worked out three times a day! Jordan called upon the expertise of a weight trainer, nutritionist, stretching coach, shooting instructor and conditioning specialist. He was determined to get the most out of his natural talents.

Several other players were probably faster than Jordan, many stronger, a few who could jump higher and definitely some better pure shooters. But no one worked as intentionally as Jordan did to put it all together. And as a result, there were no better scorers in the game. Jordan was also named to the All-Defensive First Team nine times in his illustrious career.

For every Jordan, there are dozens of flashes in the pan. Great talents who tease us with momentary glimpses of brilliance, but who never fulfill their true potential for greatness. For me, Marlon Brando immediately comes to mind.

Brando exploded onto the scene as Stanley Kowalski in *A Streetcar Named Desire.* He followed that incredible performance with *On the Waterfront.* For the next 20 to 25 years, *Streetcar* and *On the Waterfront* were arguably the best we would ever get from Brando. It's not that he stopped making films; it's just that what he did give us was mostly garbage.

His credits during those subsequent years included such ill-fated, dud films as *Guys and Dolls, The Chase, A Countess from Hong Kong, The Night of the Following Day, The Appaloosa,* and *One-Eyed Jacks.*

In 1972, Brando briefly revived his career as Don Corleone in *The Godfather.* But the sunset of his career was again marred by embarrassingly poor performances in such forgettable films as *Superman, The Brave* and *The Island of Dr. Moreau.* In July 2004 Brando died, sadly, a caricature of himself, having ballooned to over 300 pounds and essentially living as an eccentric recluse.

Why did this handsome, incredibly gifted talent disappoint us so often? Because Brando lacked the discipline necessary to develop his special talent. Brando was notoriously lazy and difficult to work with. As an example, Brando showed up for the filming of *Apocalypse Now* so obese that many of his scenes had to be cut and those that were filmed had to be shot in the dark or with dark shadows in order to conceal his obesity.

HOW TO DEVELOP YOUR TALENT

Let me offer a strategy for approaching the development of your special talents. First, define the arena in which you are playing. Is it law? If so, what is the specific discipline? Corporate law? Divorce law? Trusts and estates? Each discipline requires a very specific set of skills.

Second, make a list of every skill or talent you must develop to become a superstar in this area. It is important that you make your list detailed. By defining visually all of the areas in which we need to grow, we can craft a strategy for developing each skill. It has been my experience that if we keep it all in our head, the best we can hope for is a vague sense of what we need to do to become our best. Consequently, our strategies and execution will in all likelihood fall short. If you are serious, WRITE IT DOWN! Following I have laid out the diagram I use for my own skill development.

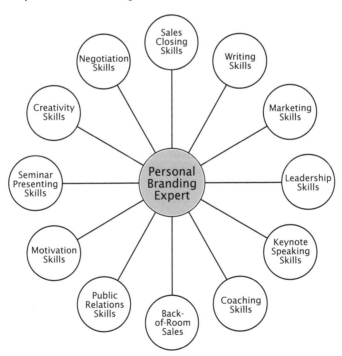

Skill Development Paradigm

The third step is to describe in detail what excellence looks like in each area. As an example, I'll illustrate my point by showing you the process I used to flesh out what excellence looks like within the discipline of keynote speaking.

KEYNOTE SPEAKING

To be a superstar at keynote speaking, I must excel in:

- Selecting a compelling topic

- Writing a great speech

- Delivering an inspiring speech

- Using my space (e.g., the stage) to its fullest

- Using drama to enhance my speech

- Cleverly using props in my presentation

- Usefully involving the audience

- Enhancing my storytelling capabilities

- Improving my use of humor

- Shocking, inspiring and helping my audience feel empathy

You can see that my description of excellence within the category of keynote speaking is extremely detailed. This is exactly how we must approach our growth and development if we want to reach our full potential.

Lastly, it is impossible to develop into a superstar on our own. I repeat: *There is no way to do it alone.* We must hire coaches. Notice I didn't say *coach;* I said *coaches.*

For example, I have retained the services of a psychologist to help me improve my one-on-one communication skills, a public speaking coach, a sales coach, a coach who specifically helps me influence professionals to sign up for our Rainmaker U. program during our public seminars, a coach with expertise in back-of-the-room product sales and a coach to help me market my keynote speeches. This list is by no means complete, but I think you get my point.

So what has been the result of all this coaching? In the training business, only 5 percent of professionals earn more than $40,000 annually. Today, due to my expertise and that of my team's coaches, we have been able to slice years off of our learning curves. Our company is now in the top 1 percent of all income earners in our profession.

A client of mine once shared with me his philosophy on coaching, which instantly changed the way I approach it myself. He told me that when he identifies an area of weakness that he needs to improve, he seeks out the person whom he perceives to be *the* expert in that area and hires him, regardless of price.

This is exactly what my team and I did when it came time to learn how to market my keynote speaking ability. I looked and looked until I found a professional in my industry who delivers more than 100 keynote speeches a year. Once I found this guy, we hired him, no questions asked.

We flew him in from Pittsburgh to Los Angeles, put him up in a five-star hotel and paid him $5,000 for a total of three hours of coaching. Might seem like a lot of money, but we knew the payoff would be huge. And it has been.

IT TAKES MORE THAN TALENT TO BE A SUPERSTAR

Talent alone will not get the job done. There are legions of talented people who, though famous, have little or no influence to mobilize others and drive positive change.

Look at Donald Trump. He is all over television and worth hundreds of millions of dollars, but few would recognize him as an example of a great personal brand. Trump is a legend in his own mind.

Your initial instinct may be to disagree with me about Trump because of his hit show, *The Apprentice,* wherein he is paid millions of dollars to utter, "You're fired." But you must remember, superstars are not just famous people who make a lot of money. Superstars inspire others to action and drive positive change. When it comes to Donald Trump, inspiration and positive change just don't come to mind.

The battle for viewership that is raging between cable networks CNN, CNBC and FOX News on the one hand and the primetime news programs on CBS, NBC and ABC on the other amplifies the point that talent alone is not enough to carry the day.

ABC, CBS and NBC all have brilliant TV journalists. So does FOX News. Like them or not, Bill O'Reilly, Sean Hannity and Brit Hume are all talented television reporters, capable of analyzing the issues, intelligently questioning guests and effectively presenting viewpoints. But they also have something their network counterparts are missing—personal brand appeal.

O'Reilly is *confrontational,* Hannity is *tenacious* and Hume is *trustworthy.* Nearing the end of their careers, Brokaw, Rather and Jennings' personal brands were growing *bland.* Argue if you want, but the ratings were irrefutable.

When they were the only news programs in town, Brokaw, Rather and Jennings commanded massive viewership numbers. Once the cable networks offered an alternative, talent was no longer enough to retain the public's loyalty. The major flagship news programs' numbers began to erode.

At first, the networks' arrogance would not allow them to admit that cable news programs were kicking their butts up and down Madison Avenue. As far as The Big Three were concerned, cable news was tabloid TV, akin to *A Current Affair.*

It has taken some brutal statistics to wake ABC, CBS and NBC up. Today, they are scrambling to find their footing. Brokaw retired gracefully, Rather was forced out and, sadly, Peter Jennings passed away of lung cancer.

If you look at the current anchors on the evening news programs, all three—ABC, CBS and NBC—have made their commitments to the future. CBS has hired Katie Couric to replace Dan Rather, while NBC selected Brian Williams to replace Tom Brokaw, and Charles Gibson has been tapped as the new face of ABC's *World News Tonight*.

While very capable, Williams lacks the pizzazz to compete with the bigger brands on the cable shows. CBS just lured Katie Couric away from *The Today Show* in hopes that her personal brand will revive its *Evening News* program. It's still too early to tell what Katie's impact will be.

ABC's choice of Gibson, while from a news reporting perspective is an excellent choice, as best I can tell, the public isn't flocking to his program.

Here's a suggestion for the head honchos at CBS, NBC and ABC: *stuffy*, *stiff* and *vanilla* don't work. The people want substance packaged with style. Even if most people are not formally educated, they don't need to be told what's important. Stop giving them what you think they need and start giving them what they want.

Choose entertaining commentators and report on stories that highlight traditional values, like hard work, decency and respect for faith and country, and you'll regain the numbers you enjoyed in your glory years. Ignore what the people want and the best you can hope for is slow erosion until you quietly slip away into irrelevance.

CHAPTER SUMMARY

Key Points

- ■ We must have a high level of skill if we hope to deliver on our promises to perform.
- ■ The strategy for talent development:
  - • Select an area of focus (e.g., public speaking).
  - • Identify every skill or talent you must develop in order to become a superstar performer in that area.
  - • Describe what excellence looks like within each narrow category.
  - • Go to work! Pursue excellence with discipline that borders on addiction.
- ■ Remember, talent alone will not make us a superstar in our industry.

Part
TWO

Building Your Own Personal Brand

EIGHT

Strive for Greatness, Not Power

There is a huge difference between a great personal brand and a powerful one. A great personal brand bespeaks honor and inspires others to action. A powerful personal brand derives its influence from fear and commands action through intimidation. Churchill and Roosevelt had great personal brands. Stalin and Hitler had powerful ones.

Leaders obsessed with building a powerful personal brand are typically detached from reality and rarely have any idea of their personal brand's shortcomings. They intentionally surround themselves with minions who praise their every move. It is not unusual for the powerful to think they are great.

A client was recently telling me about a CEO of a Fortune 500 insurance company who attended his company's annual black-tie gala wearing a purple tuxedo jacket. Purple! What made this faux pas especially ridiculous was that this CEO had gone to great lengths to ensure that everyone else in the company wore only traditional black-tie attire. How, you may wonder, could this guy be so out of touch with reality to not see the absurdity of his behavior? The answer is revealed in the words of the great British historian Lord Acton: "Power corrupts. Absolute power corrupts absolutely."

We see this same type of arrogance today with professional athletes, entertainers and celebrity CEOs. Having a lot of money or fame does not guarantee greatness. We all know legions of famous people who have lots of money whom we would hardly describe as having a great personal brand. Here are three: Michael Jackson, Kenneth Lay and Dennis Rodman. People don't like jerks, liars and braggarts.

I have found that there are three characteristics people admire: honor, authenticity and gratitude. Build your personal brand on these foundational principles and your appeal will be enduring.

HONOR

When you set out to create your personal brand, shoot for honor. Honor is the bedrock upon which legacies are built. True honor requires humility of heart, dogged commitment to self-perspective and correctness and the uncompromising discipline to always do the right thing. Toward the end of President Truman's second term, his approval ratings sank to a dismal 36 percent. As his advisors began to fret about what to do, Truman calmed them, saying, "It isn't the polls and public opinion of the moment that counts. It's what's right and wrong that matters."

As I tell my clients, "Doing the difficult thing and doing the right thing is often the same thing."

Abraham Lincoln offers us an excellent example. The phrase most of us think of when we think of Lincoln is *Honest Abe*. Lincoln worked on building his personal brand long before he ever became president.

In 1835, a young and naïve Lincoln went into business with two other men. In a very short time, these partners revealed themselves to be not only poor businessmen, but alcoholics and deadbeats as well. Lincoln and his partners' business soon went belly-up. His partners quickly secreted out of town under cover of night and left Lincoln with the obligation of repaying $1,100 in debts. Lincoln had two choices: run like his partners or stay and repay his debts. Lincoln chose to stay for 11 more years until the company's debts were repaid in full. As far as Lincoln was concerned, there was no "company debt." Lincoln viewed the money owed as a personal obligation because it had been lent to him on the credibility of his name.

Lincoln's lesson to us is that we have to *be* honest for a long, long, long time before people will describe us as honest. This includes when no one else is watching.

Two years ago, I was in Maui, Hawaii, on my honeymoon. If you've ever been to Maui you know there are kiosks on just about every corner selling timeshares. On this particular day, I happened to be sitting on a bench next to one of these kiosks when a man who was obviously a tourist approached and asked the person working the kiosk for directions. Ever the salesman, the kiosk worker quickly drew the tourist into his web.

The sum of the timeshare salesman's pitch to this easy mark was, "If you just go to this one-hour presentation and just listen, we'll give you and your wife two free tickets for a sunset cruise." The salesman emphasized that there was absolutely no obligation to buy anything. All the tourist had to do was fill out an enrollment card at the kiosk and attend the presentation.

I could see the tourist's suspicions rise. "So all I have to do is fill out that card and listen to a one-hour presentation?"

"That's it," answered the salesman.

After some hemming and hawing, the tourist capitulated, "Okay, I'll do it."

"Great, just fill out this enrollment card and you'll be on your way," responded the salesman.

Together, the salesman and the tourist began to fill out the card. "Your name here, your address here, check 'yes' down here," directed the salesman.

Eventually, they got to a question that asked, "Is anyone in your family employed in the travel business?" Assuming the answer was "no," the salesman directed the tourist to strike the "no" box.

The tourist hesitated for a second and said, "Well, that's not really true."

"What do you mean?" the salesman probed.

"Well, my wife occasionally makes reservations for groups through our church," the tourist confessed.

"Oh, don't worry about it, nobody will know. Just mark 'no,'" said the salesman.

The tourist paused for a second and then said softly, "I can't do that."

"Why not?" queried the salesman.

"I'm a minister," was the response.

With that, the conversation was over. The minister thanked the salesman for his time and departed.

How many people do what is in their own best interest as opposed to what is morally right when they know they will never be caught? The honorable personal brands do what is right, not what is expedient.

AUTHENTICITY

All great brands are authentic. Authenticity begins with a true acceptance of the real you. The moment people sense we are trying to be something we are not, we're finished. Our goal in building our personal brand is to find that one thing about us that represents the essence of who we are and then build our personal brand around that quality. Make it as simple, straightforward and unambiguous as possible.

Oprah is *warm;* she's one of us. Lady Di was *caring.* Mother Teresa was the epitome of *self-sacrifice.* There is/was no pretending with any of these people. They are/were in real life exactly who they are/were depicted as in the media.

Choosing a personal brand that is not a true reflection of the real us is fraught with danger. First, it is exhausting to always have to be "on." Second, if we are successful in promoting this inauthentic personal brand, after awhile we will come to hate it because we will eventually feel like prisoners to it.

A personal brand built upon a lie will inevitably come crashing down. And when it does, the damage is usually irreparable. Take the late Rock Hudson.

Rock Hudson lived a lie his entire adult life. Millions of fans instantly fell in love with this hunk when he stepped onto the cinema stage in *Giant* as Jordan "Bick" Benedict Jr. The studios, his own handlers and Rock himself all banded together to promote Rock's personal brand as a sex symbol and lady killer. In truth, Rock Hudson was gay. But nobody wanted to tell the truth about Rock because of the damage it would do to his career.

In the end, the lie was too much. It all came crashing down in 1985 when Rock Hudson died of AIDS. Sadly, his death was ignominious, not because he died of AIDS, but rather because he had lied all those years to the fans who adored him. Instead of being remembered as the heartthrob he pretended to be, today "Rock Hudson" is the punch line of many tasteless jokes. This is not a fate that should have befallen a man who was uniformly regarded by his peers as a true gentleman.

GRATITUDE

The fastest way to turn off the people who give us their support, admiration and trust is to take them for granted. The more successful we become, the more grateful we need to be. We must never tire of showing others our gratitude, even when we are not in the mood. Every chance we get we must say "thank you," "please," "you are welcome" and "I appreciate it." Unfortunately, many who become successful forget to practice good manners.

We see this dynamic at play a lot in Hollywood. Those stars who seem to appreciate the public's support—Tom Hanks, Arnold Schwarzenegger and Mike Myers—grow bigger and bigger. They are not afraid to poke fun at themselves. One of the best when it comes to self-satire is John Travolta. Though we love him for the roles he plays today, we can never get enough of Vinnie Barbarino in *Welcome Back, Kotter* and Tony Manero in *Saturday Night Fever.* Whenever Travolta appears as a guest on late night talk shows and as the guest host on *Saturday Night Live,* he never disappoints. He always willingly goes along with the gag and we love him more and more each time. It is precisely because he is so lovable that he can survive such forgettable bombs as *White Man's Burden, The Punisher* and *Battlefield Earth.*

Then there are others who develop a sense of entitlement once they achieve movie stardom. The very same public whom they begged to love them suddenly become an irritant. We don't need to name names because we know who they are. These ingrates act like they are doing their fans a favor. The only thing that mystifies me is why anyone would put up with such disrespect.

I don't know if it is true, but I once read how JFK Jr. handled the hordes of press that followed him around daily. When he was going to an event at which he knew the press would probably want to photograph him, JFK Jr. would have his PR person call the press ahead of time and let them know where and when he would arrive so they could get all the photographs they wanted. Once they had gotten all the photos they wanted (or at least a reasonable amount), they would pretty much leave him and his guest alone for the balance of the evening.

There is rarely ever an excuse for ingratitude. Think about it: 99 percent of the time, celebrity is not forced upon people. It is typically the result of intentional choices people make. My opinion is, if you don't like all the extras that come along with celebrity, don't pursue it.

POSITIVELY GOOD, NOT PERFECT

Too often, people get bogged down in the pursuit of perfection when creating their personal brand. This is a waste of time. There is no perfect personal brand and there are no perfect words to express our personal brand. *Positively good is good enough.* Strive to create a *positively good* personal brand. We can assure you that this *positively good* personal brand will be enough to carry the day 99 percent of the time. As Canadian poet and songwriter Leonard Cohen once remarked, "Forget the perfect offering. There is a crack in everything. That is how the light gets in."

The amount of time and energy it takes to go from positively good to perfection is extraordinary, but the benefits are negligible. It's very rare that clients will even notice the extra effort or that it will translate into any meaningful return on our investment. In most instances, only we truly appreciate our obsession with perfection.

Do not torture yourself trying to come up with the perfect personal brand. If you become a prisoner to perfection, you will never be satisfied with your personal brand and, consequently, you will never experience the fun and joy of building and marketing a truly great personal brand.

I was recently reading Rainer Maria Rilke's *Letters to a Young Poet* and came across a wonderful passage that illustrates this point beautifully. Rilke was an accomplished German poet, and *Letters* is a compilation of letters he wrote to a young, aspiring poet, in which Rilke shares what he believes it takes to be a great poet. Among the many sagacious words of advice offered by Rilke, to me one point stood out above all the rest. Rilke told the young man, "A masterpiece is never finished. At some point it must be abandoned."

I am sure Michelangelo could have found numerous ways to improve upon the *Sistine Chapel* or da Vinci the *Mona Lisa,* but at some point they had to say, "I'm finished." Had they not, these magnificent artists may never have gone on to create all of the other wonderful masterpieces they gave us.

Think simple, straightforward, unambiguous. Pick one quality and work unceasingly to be known for that quality. President Truman was a *simple man,* President Kennedy is remembered for *style,* and President Reagan was the *great communicator.* Surely there were many more dimensions to these men, but it was that one single quality that won them their historical acclaim.

CHAPTER SUMMARY

Key Points

- Strive for greatness—not power.
- Seek honor—not fame. Honor is fame with glory.
- The best brands are the most authentic.
- Live life with an attitude of gratitude and you'll have all you ever wanted.
- Remember, be positively good—don't try to be perfect.

NINE

Building Your Own Personal Brand

When choosing our personal brand, we need to follow five key steps:

1. Select the right domain
2. Identify all of our personal descriptive qualities
3. Crystallize the benefits those qualities provide our audience
4. Pick one benefit upon which to build our personal brand
5. If appropriate, turn that benefit into a catchy phrase

STEP ONE: SELECTING THE RIGHT DOMAIN FOR YOU

Correctly defining our target audience is the first step we must take when identifying our personal brand. The reason should be obvious: We have to know *to whom* we are selling before we can decide *what* we are selling them. In his book *The Personal Branding Phenomenon,* Peter Montoya refers to this process as "identifying your domain." Just like the lion is king of his domain (i.e., the jungle), our objective should be to position ourselves as the king (or queen) of our own specific domain. We accomplish dominance by properly defining our target market and then saturating that market with our message until we and our message are top of mind.

Start asking yourself questions like, "Where do I want to be influential?" "With whom will my message resonate?" "If I could pick the perfect audience, what would it look like and where would I find a high concentration of these people?"

A very common mistake professionals make when defining their domain is defining it too broadly. The pitfalls of this error are three-fold.

Pitfall #1: Dilution of Your Message

The broader our domain, the more ground we have to cover and, hence, the more diluted our message will be by the time it reaches the ears of our target audience.

Financial advisors and life insurance brokers are two groups of professionals whom I have found sometimes define their target audience too broadly. It is not uncommon for a financial advisor or insurance broker working in Los Angeles to enter Rainmaker U. with the following target audience: *high-net-worth individuals.*

There are currently 3 million people living in the city of Los Angeles and 20 million living in Los Angeles County. The median price of a home in L.A. County is $500,000. If it were its own country, L.A. County would have the 12th largest GNP in the world!

Literally hundreds of thousands of people and households spread out all across the city and county fall within the broad criteria of *high-net-worth individuals.* There is absolutely no way a financial advisor or life insurance broker, absent the extraordinary resources necessary to run a sustained print, radio and television media campaign, could effectively communicate his message to this target audience.

We must shrink our focus down so that our message is hitting our target audience like a battering ram while the message of our competitors, who are all over the place, falls upon the same target audience like a light mist. If I could command you to do one thing in this brand selection process, it would be this: *Think intelligently about whom* exactly *you want to reach, where the greatest concentration of this group is, and then figure out how you can reach them most efficiently.*

Pitfall #2: Spreading Your Resources Too Thin

Many of us do not have unlimited resources. We have only so much time, money and customer service capability. Professionals who define their domains too broadly usually end up spreading themselves too thin, spending their days like pinballs bouncing up and down, side to side, in an effort to cover their entire target audience.

For example, suppose you were a financial advisor and you wanted to do a mailing announcing a new product or service to every individual in the city of Los Angeles who earns $500,000 or more per year. In a city with a population of more than 3 million, that could easily be more than 100,000 people! You can just imagine the financial cost of such a project. Even if you were to do a one-time mailing of 100,000 pieces, how effective do you think it would be?

Studies show that the average person has to hear another person's message six to eight times to remember that person. In other words, our mailings are pretty much useless unless we intend to replicate this strategy five to seven more times.

I know a lawyer who mails out literally thousands of computer-generated form letters once a year to every person he has in his database, telling them of his most recent successes. Twelve months later he does the same thing, and so on and so on. If we are to believe the statistics, this would seem to be a waste of time and money, not to mention paper!

Wouldn't it be so much more efficient and economical to target just 2,500 or even 1,000 qualified prospects and commit to first-rate contact with each of them?

Pitfall #3: The Scarcity Mindset

Professionals who define their domain as broadly as possible usually do so in order to ensure they don't miss out on even one single opportunity. This strategy is usually the by-product of a scarcity mindset. The scarcity crowd fears that there are so few opportunities out there that they cannot afford to miss even one deal, no matter how small.

One of my clients, a top salesman with a top insurance company, used to embrace this strategy. Before we started working together, his target audience was any attorney earning $250,000 or more. But, he was also quick to add, "Of course, if you know of *anyone* who is in the market for insurance, I'd love to talk to them as well." Not only did this strategy have him running all over the city, it certainly watered down the cache of his personal brand.

Another client, Brad Lyon, a business manager in Los Angeles, is the best in the business as far as I am concerned. For the past 12 months, I have been wrestling with him to get him to redefine his target audience more narrowly. Right now, he focuses on individuals and households earning $250,000 or more per year. Like my insurance agent client, Brad might as well be randomly casting his line into the Pacific Ocean. I know his client base includes a lot of entertainment executives, so I recently asked Brad, "What if you focused on just entertainment executives earning $250,000? Is there enough opportunity for you?"

Without hesitation, Brad responded, "Absolutely." My suggestion to Brad was to position himself as *The Person to See* within the entertainment executive community. Things would be so much easier.

By now you probably have a sense of where I am headed. When defining your domain, think narrow. Our long-term objective should be narrow and deep. The maturing of my own business development strategy is a perfect example.

Our initial strategy was to target anyone earning $200,000 a year anywhere we found them. After a year of spraying and praying from city to city, county to county and—believe it or not—state to state, we realized we had to readjust our focus. Because industry diversity is important to our program, we needed more than one target audience. We decided to confine our efforts to five industries: lawyers, accountants, financial advisors, insurance and commercial real estate. Better, but still too broad.

A year later, we narrowed our focus even more. We decided to pick three zip codes in downtown Los Angeles (90010, 90017 and 90071) and saturate that market with our message until every professional in these three zip codes earning $200,000 or more knows what Rainmaker U. is and why they cannot afford to not participate in our program. Our team is now focused like a laser. I am more excited about market domination than ever before.

Domain Selection: A Recommendation

The strategy we recommend our clients use when defining their domain is the "10/50" rule. We encourage our clients to choose a target audience large enough that if they were able to capture 10 percent of the total market share of that market, they would not be able to handle all of the business they generated. The "50" stands for the proposition that they should not look to redefine or expand the definition of their target audience until they have captured 50 percent of that market. In other words, don't move on to new fields until you've harvested all you can from the one you've initially defined for yourself.

The mistake many people make as soon as they start having some success within their initially defined target market is to expand outside that market before capturing anywhere near 50 percent of the total market share opportunity. We call this the "Donna Karan Syndrome."

Do you remember what Donna Karan's brand was when she arrived on the scene in the 80s? High-end women's clothing. Donna Karan quickly exploded as *the* brand in which stylish women wanted to be seen. What she did next virtually destroyed all of the cache her brand had developed. Donna Karan made the mistake of watering down her brand with line extensions. She went nuts putting her personal brand on everything from umbrellas to men's underwear.

Once you start racking up the successes, go deeper—not wider. Guard against taking the advice of friends, family and employees who encourage you to expand your focus prematurely. Think of yourself as an early American Christian evangelist. Their mission was to go from town to town converting the non-believers. Their strategy was to remain in that town until a critical, self-sustaining mass had been converted and only then would they move on to the next town.

Key Domain Criteria

It's time for some specific, concrete ideas about the criteria you may want to consider when defining your own domain. As we at The Personal Branding Group did, you too can define your domain by geographical boundaries. Los Angeles is a big city with a lot of professionals who earn $200,000 or more per year. They are downtown (in the 90010, 90017 and 90071 zip codes), on the Westside, in the South Bay and in the Valley. Have the courage to make the tough choices. Where would it be most productive to spend most of your time?

Maybe you want to focus on businesses with a certain employee or revenue size. We try to get many of our clients to focus on specific industries (e.g., accountants, lawyers or real estate professionals). How much more efficient would your marketing be if you could successfully position yourself as *The Accountant to See for litigation attorneys in your town,* versus the accountant who is running around the city like a chicken with his head cut off, trying to sign up every client he can?

One of my clients, Kevin Brennan, is a top-flight tenant broker in San Francisco with the commercial brokerage firm Studley, Inc. For years Kevin has been chasing deals all over the city across industry lines. Even though Kevin has been very successful, he was convinced he could do better if he would just develop better focus. After some brainstorming, Kevin and I decided that he and his team should focus exclusively on law firms needing 20,000 or more feet of space. Kevin and his team have been re-energized and are off to the races.

There are, of course, some instances where we may actually be defining our target market too narrowly. Another client of ours, Anthony Marguleas, is the owner of Amalfi Estates, a residential real estate company that focuses on the Pacific Palisades section of Los Angeles. For 10 years, Anthony represented buyers only. While this strategy did enable Anthony to carve out a niche for himself and his firm, he was also foregoing hundreds of thousands of dollars in listing revenues.

Even more problematic for Anthony was losing great agents to other companies because of his decision to not represent sellers. After one of his best agents left Amalfi because of this limitation, Anthony did some deep soul searching on the practicalities of his buyers-only strategy. Eventually, Anthony re-branded his company as a full-service residential real estate firm representing both buyers and sellers. As a result, Anthony's business exploded. This year alone his business has more than tripled to over $100 million in sales.

One of the most compelling examples of smart domain selection I've come across is Tom Gossen's. I stumbled upon Tom's flyer while at my printer, Michael Zokai's office. It was brilliant. The flyer was just 4" x 11" with a picture of Tom's smiling face smack-dab in the middle, with only his telephone number printed under it. Above his picture were four simple words: "THE GAY MAN'S THERAPIST." Now that's focus.

Think about it. If Tom got even 1 percent of all of the business in Los Angeles, he would be overwhelmed. The only suggestion we might have for Tom would be to focus even more narrowly (e.g., gay lawyers on the Westside of Los Angeles over 40 years old).

Below are some examples of domains we helped our clients select during their involvement in Rainmaker U. Notice the singularity of focus of each:

- A lawyer focused on defending entertainment lawyers who've been sued for malpractice.
- A residential real estate broker focused on luxury homes in Pacific Palisades, California.
- A Jewish insurance broker focused on writing insurance for Jews in Beverly Hills with a net worth of $1 million or more.
- A financial advisor focused on corporate lawyers on the Westside.
- A strategic business advisor focused on commercial real estate brokers earning $250,000 or more in downtown Los Angeles.
- A residential mortgage broker focused on writing Jumbo mortgages ($500,000 or more) for television actors and actresses.
- A business consultant focused on non-profit, private secondary education schools (i.e., high schools).
- An employee benefits insurance broker focused on managing partners of law firms.
- A real estate investment fund focused on CEOs of publicly traded companies in the western United States.
- A commercial insurance agent focused on non-profit associations in the San Fernando Valley.
- A life insurance agent focused on family-owned offices in Los Angeles.
- A sales trainer focused on new insurance brokers with insurance companies in Los Angeles.

What makes these domains so effective is that our clients had the courage to think and act narrowly. They weren't afraid to give up opportunity outside of their narrowly defined domain because they realized the greater value of focusing all of their efforts within the boundaries they had set for themselves. So far, the results have been excellent.

One client recently informed me that because of his laser-like focus, he grew his business in two short years from $2.5 million to $4.3 million. He also told me his quality of life is much better because he is not zigzagging all over the place chasing every opportunity that comes across his desk.

STEP TWO: PERSONAL DESCRIPTIVE QUALITIES

Now that we know to whom we are selling, it's time for the fun part: going through the process of actually crystallizing our new personal brand. Let's remember the overall objective of our work in this section: **To choose an authentic personal brand that represents the value or quality we want others to think of when they think of us.**

As we work through steps two, three and four of this process, there are several points we need to keep in mind. First, our personal brand is about who we are personally as opposed to what we do for a living. First Lady Laura Bush is known for her *class*, Tom Hanks for his *guy-next-door* persona and Brett Favre for his *toughness*. Sometimes people make the mistake of confusing what they are known for in their profession with what they think their personal brand should be.

For example, I have a client in the commercial real estate finance industry who kept insisting that his personal brand was *the go-to guy when it came to commercial real estate finance*. After some coaching, he came to understand that *the go-to guy in the commercial real estate industry* was merely the arena in which he was promoting his personal brand. He still needed to identify that human quality that defines him most favorably with his target audience.

We should also be sure to choose a personal brand that is relevant to our target audience. Suppose commercial litigation is the forum in which we are performing. If we want to attract a lot of business, we must promote a quality about ourselves that is compelling to our target audience. What do successful businesspeople who hire a litigator want? *Kind? Easygoing? Generous?* Though certainly admirable, these are probably not the qualities clients are looking for when they find themselves in a bind. More than likely, folks want *smarts, tenacity* and *a winner.*

Every now and again, I run into clients who insist on building their personal brand on a quality about themselves that they are in love with, but which has no relevancy to their target audience. Usually these people defend their choice by saying, "This is who I am, and if others don't like me there is nothing I can do about it." This approach violates the first rule of personal branding: *Personal branding has nothing to do with what you think about yourself and everything to do with what your target audience **feels** about you.*

I also sometimes run into someone who resists personal branding because he "refuses to pretend he is something he is not." If rule number one is *what they **feel** matters*, rule number two is *authenticity.* Never build a personal brand on something you are not. To borrow from Zig Ziglar, your personal brand must be "a true reflection of the real you."

Say what you want about Barry Bonds; he is *authentic.* What you see is what you get: a rude, in-your-face egomaniac. Contrast that with Kirby Puckett, the superstar center fielder for the Minnesota Twins in the '80s and early '90s. To say he was beloved by the state of Minnesota in his playing days is an understatement. Kirby was, or at least he appeared to be, everything today's self-centered superstar is not: a loyal, decent family man, upstanding citizen of the community, honest, hardworking and a team player. Kirby did not need the mayor of the Twin Cities to give him the keys to the city because Kirby owned the whole state. His personal brand equity reached its zenith when he was forced to leave the game prematurely because of a degenerative eye disease.

Kirby worked hard to cultivate this *all-around good guy* personal brand and was very successful up until "Kirbygate" broke in 2002. That year, Minnesota's favorite son went on trial for sexual assault. Initially, the public was outraged that Kirby was being unfairly accused. But then the truth came out. Kirby Puckett was exposed as a serial womanizer who regularly cheated on his wife and abused women. His fall from grace was swift.

Remember U.S. Senator Strom Thurmond of South Carolina? Senator Thurmond was an ardent segregationist who once ran for the presidency on a platform of "Segregation Now and Forever." The only problem was good, old Senator Thurmond secretly fathered a daughter out of wedlock with the Thurmond family's black maid! To make matters worse, Senator Thurmond kept his hypocrisy silent until the truth was exposed posthumously.

Building our personal brand on a lie is also exhausting because we always have to be "on." When we are in a good mood and things are going our way, being "on" is easy, but when times get tough, being "on" is much more difficult. The problem with being "on" is we leave ourselves with no choice. Our "on" persona brings with it certain expectations. And we must either fulfill those expectations or run the risk of undermining all the personal brand equity we have worked so hard to build up.

I think my own personality offers a good example of the point I'm trying to make. For the most part, I have a positive, upbeat, can-do attitude. I enjoy people and I love trying to help them be better.

It is not unusual for a client to ask me, "Do you ever get tired of being *on?*" My answer is always the same: "No, because I'm not *on.* I'm just me."

Here's an example of what I'm talking about when I say "on." A friend of mine recently played in a charity golf tournament with a well-known pro on the PGA Tour. My friend, who paid a lot of money to play with this professional, told me that when the cameras weren't on, this guy barely talked to him.

On the 16th hole, however, my friend hit his ball into the water. A cameraman happened to be nearby so the camera crew came over to capture this golf professional helping his amateur partner (my buddy) find his ball. Instantly, Mr. Ice transformed himself into Wally Cleaver, putting his arm around my friend's shoulder while they searched for my friend's ball. When the camera turned off, so did the charm.

Where to Start: Creating the Foundation

When crystallizing our personal brand, regardless of job title, net income or industry, we all start in the same place—by building a rock-solid foundation. We must have a solid foundation upon which to build our personal brand or else it will collapse when we are confronted with adversity.

In creating a personal brand, our foundation is our descriptive human qualities. Are you tall? Short? Athletic? Intelligent, charismatic or motivated? Are you tough? Outgoing? A Harvard grad or former college ballplayer?

The metaphor that comes to mind when I think of descriptive qualities is Legos. Do you remember playing with Legos as a child? There were so many different colors: white, blue, black, green, yellow, etc. Our descriptive qualities are like our Legos. Each color represents a specific quality.

The individual Lego pieces spread out on the floor represent nothing. However, when they are manipulated, stacked and combined a certain way—presto! They become whatever we want them to be: a truck, tall building or bridge. We build our personal brand in exactly the same way, by playing with our descriptive qualities until they communicate something special to our target audience.

When identifying your descriptive characteristics, keep in mind: (1) It's all about you, (2) the characteristics you list must be relevant to your target audience and (3) there is no room for modesty. The great American poet Robert Frost once remarked, "No passion in the writer, no passion in the reader." Similarly, if you are not excited about who you are, why should your target audience be?

Your list of descriptive qualities must be an exhaustive reflection of all aspects of your character. Describe everything about who you are as a human being. Your list could include components of your physicality, intellect, personality, background, education, likes, quirks, interests.

We also encourage you to list each quality with any superlatives you think apply. Again, cast aside bashfulness. Are you a super motivator? A genius? Incredibly funny? Tough as nails? Don't worry about sounding conceited. Your list is for you and those colleagues who are committed to your success.

Let's take time now to analyze some of the descriptive qualities of a couple of well-known, respected personalities.

Lance Armstrong		
■ Proven winner	■ Very charismatic	■ Mentally tough
■ Cancer survivor	■ In-your-face attitude	■ Super wealthy
■ Fierce competitor	■ Outspoken	■ Incredibly disciplined
■ World-class athlete	■ Late bloomer	■ Very charitable
■ Physically powerful	■ Father	■ Handsome

Oprah Winfrey		
■ Incredibly successful	■ Full-figured	■ Ambitious
■ Unbelievably generous	■ Articulate	■ Great one-on-one interviewer
■ Survivor	■ Genuine	■ Outspoken
■ Marketing genius	■ Incredibly influential	■ Gifted public speaker
■ Super wealthy	■ Elegant	■ Great sense of humor
■ Pretty	■ Very human/ real	■ Fiercely independent
■ Woman	■ Leader	

The above lists are by no means exhaustive, but rather simply descriptive qualities I have discerned using my own observations. If you want to get a sense of the real Lance Armstrong, I suggest you start with his autobiography *It's Not About the Bike.* For Oprah, pick up *The Uncommon Wisdom of Oprah Winfrey: A Portrait in Her Own Words.*

Below are some of my own descriptive qualities. I've included them because it might be a bit easier to relate to me and my personal brand than to the personal brands of mega-superstars.

Tim O'Brien		
▪ Lawyer ▪ Very charismatic ▪ Great motivator ▪ Very caring ▪ Innovative ▪ Incredible tenacity ▪ Extremely passionate ▪ Powerful perseverance	▪ Georgetown law graduate ▪ Exceptional public speaker ▪ Excellent instincts ▪ First-rate people skills ▪ Nice looking ▪ Extremely informed ▪ Knowledgeable on personal branding	▪ Strong sense of self ▪ Very blunt communicator ▪ Highly ethical ▪ Stubborn ▪ Very ambitious ▪ Unbelievably driven ▪ Very generous ▪ Passionate

When you first read my list of descriptive qualities, your reaction might be, "Man, this guy is an egomaniac." Remember, my list *should* be very complimentary. It's a litany of my most positive qualities. (I assure you that, if given the chance, I could come up with an equally impressive list of shortcomings.)

Every one of us should be in a healthy love affair with ourselves. That doesn't mean to become self-obsessed or self-satisfied. In fact, it means the exact opposite. We should care so much about ourselves that we are constantly looking for ways to improve and grow.

My list was compiled with the help of family and colleagues. I wanted to be sure that the qualities I identified were realistic, accurate and relevant. Some of the qualities I initially listed I ended up crossing off at the urging of my peers. Some that made the final cut were added at my peers' suggestion.

Here's an exercise that may help you as you approach this part of the personal branding process. I know it has been a big help to me. Close your eyes and recall a time when you felt you were at your best. I want you to fully associate back to that time as if you are living it all over again. As you do, notice all of the positive qualities you observe in yourself. I want you to visualize as many scenarios as you need to, until you are satisfied that you have made an exhaustive list of the best of you.

In a perfect world, I'd love for you to engage in this process with a mini handheld tape recorder, which would allow you to narrate in real time what you are observing about yourself. If you don't have a handheld recorder, just have paper and pen ready so that, after each visualization, you can open your eyes and record each of the descriptive qualities you observed.

When I did this exercise, I visualized myself in a competitive situation playing college basketball. The best game of my modest career was in 1988, against Mount St. Mary's, the Division II NCAA National Champion (I played for Catholic University, which was Division III). That year, we upset the Mount. As I closed my eyes and observed myself, the picture that popped into my mind was me playing tenacious defense. Satisfied that *incredible tenacity* was the appropriate descriptive quality, I opened my eyes and jotted it down. I did this over and over again until I had compiled an exhaustive list of all of my best qualities. It's kind of like shaking an apple tree until all of the ripe apples have fallen to the ground.

On page 129 is a blank worksheet that you can use right now to make a detailed list of all of your best descriptive qualities. To help reinforce in your mind that each of these qualities is, in fact, a true reflection of the real you, I want you to write down specific evidence that proves to you that you possess this quality. Below is an example of a worksheet one of my clients filled out.

Descriptive Qualities Worksheet	
Michael Quinn	
QUALITY	EVIDENCE
■ Incredibly tenacious	■ In one year went from last to first in production
■ Devout Catholic	■ Daily communicant
■ Financially savvy	■ $2M net worth by 30
■ Compassionate	■ Gives away 10 percent of wealth
■ Great listener	■ Never interrupts
■ Unbelievably hungry to learn/succeed	■ Spends $50–75K/year on coaching
■ Hustler	■ Works 14-hour days
■ Focused beyond belief	■ Measures daily activity level religiously
■ Proven track record	■ Number six in company (nationally) after just six years

Now it's time for you to do the same. A blank *Descriptive Qualities Worksheet* is just waiting for you on the next page. Remember the adage, "The best intention no matter how strong, diminishes over time." If you don't do this exercise right now, it is unlikely that you ever will.

Descriptive Qualities Worksheet

(name)

QUALITY	EVIDENCE

Next, send your *Descriptive Qualities Worksheet* to three trusted colleagues and ask them to critique what you've written. It is absolutely essential that you choose people who are not afraid to tell you the truth. Your success in this process depends upon your peers' brutal honesty.

Your instructions to your reviewers should be specific. They are free to cross out any of the descriptive qualities you've identified, modify the backup evidence you've referenced and, most important, they should feel free to add to your list based upon their own interactions with you. It is not unusual for us to omit a positive descriptive quality because modesty gets the best of us.

On the following page is an example of how I might edit Michael Quinn's *Descriptive Qualities Worksheet* if I were a colleague. While *devout Catholic* is noble, and obviously very important to Michael, it is probably not relevant to his target audience.

Once you've compiled your list and collected constructive feedback from your trusted peers, you are ready to begin shaping and molding your personal brand.

STEP THREE: THE BENEFITS

There is an old sales saying: "Features tell; benefits sell." In other words, people buy benefits, not features. For example, a feature of a computer software package may be a spam blocker. While this feature may sound enticing, we will probably be even more excited and more likely to purchase the product if we know what specifically it can do for us. In other words, what is the quantifiable benefit *we* get if we buy this spam blocker? Does this spam-blocking feature offer us the benefit of reducing spam by 80 percent? Will it save us time and, if so, how much? Can we customize which kind of spam we want to keep out? The buyer needs to know exactly what's in it for him before he will be excited enough to buy it.

The same psychology applies to our personal brand. People will only be attracted to our personal brand if there is something specific in

Descriptive Qualities Worksheet	
Michael Quinn	
QUALITY	EVIDENCE
• Incredibly tenacious	• In one year went from last to first in production
• ~~Devout Catholic~~	• ~~Daily communicant~~
• Financially savvy	• $2M net worth by 30
• Compassionate	• Gives away 10 percent of wealth
• Great listener	• Never interrupts
• Unbelievably hungry to learn/succeed	• Spends $50–75K/year on coaching
• Hustler	• Works 14-hour days
• Focused beyond belief	• Measures daily activity level religiously
• Proven track record	• Number six in company (nationally) after just six years

our brand for them. Take Lance Armstrong. His personal brand is *winner*. We are attracted to his personal brand because we are inspired and motivated by him. We want to be a *winner* just like Lance.

George W. Bush won the 2004 election because his personal brand was a *strong leader*. In these uncertain times, President Bush made the electorate feel safer than John Kerry did. In contrast, George H. W. Bush lost the 1992 election to Bill Clinton because he didn't give the electorate something compelling to buy. The knock on Bush was he lacked "the vision thing."

The bottom line is, if we want our personal brand to sell, it must offer our target audience something our target audience wants. Is it *trust? Excellence? Extraordinary customer service?* Whatever we select, our ambition should be to become the epitome of that quality (e.g., when I think of *trust* in commercial real estate, Dave Kinney is the first person to come to mind).

Now it's time to manipulate, play with and possibly combine our descriptive qualities in order to discover the benefits they might offer our target audience. Sometimes an individual descriptive quality by itself is the value or quality we want to promote. Other times we may need to combine two or more descriptive qualities to fully communicate the benefit or value we want to promote.

Brett Favre's personal brand is an example of how sometimes the right personal brand may reveal itself in the list of descriptive qualities.

As we examine Brett's descriptive qualities, several immediately jump out as possible personal brand choices: *great leader, fiercely competitive, incredibly tough.* Each of these qualities creates strong emotions within us. People love Brett Favre because he is a *great leader, fiercely competitive, incredibly tough.* The more authentic the choice, the more vivid the images will be in Brett's target audience's mind and thus the stronger their emotions will be. When confronted with the challenge of selecting from several good choices, the right strategy is to look for uniqueness.

Of all of Brett Favre's qualities, *incredibly tough* would probably be the most unique personal brand because of the powerful evidence he has to back it up. Favre is a quarterback, and quarterbacks are sometimes perceived as prima donnas. The NFL has created all kinds of rules to protect them from getting hit too often and too hard during games. During practice, quarterbacks wear special yellow jerseys, which signal to everyone else that hitting the quarterback is off-limits.

No one who knows Brett Favre would ever accuse him of being a prima donna. He has, by far, the longest consecutive game-playing streak of any quarterback in the history of the NFL, having started 237 consecutive games and counting. The next closest player is Indianapolis Colts quarterback Peyton Manning, with 144 consecutive games under his belt.

Descriptive Qualities Worksheet	
Brett Favre	
QUALITY	EVIDENCE
▪ Dynamic personality	▪ Everybody loves him— teammates and town
▪ Incredibly tough	▪ Started in 237 consecutive games—longest in history
▪ Winner	▪ Won one Super Bowl; went to second; was the NFL's MVP three times
▪ Loyal teammate	▪ Never talks bad about anyone; never blames anyone but self for loss
▪ Loving husband/father	▪ Quit drinking and carousing to save his family
▪ Extraordinarily talented	▪ The only three-time MVP winner in NFL history
▪ Incredibly funny	▪ Great practical joker; networks love to put mic on him on game day
▪ Fierce competitor	▪ Played with concussion, broken ribs, broken thumb, etc.
▪ Super leader	▪ Brett Favre is Mr. Green Bay Packer

Favre has played through concussions, a broken thumb, broken ribs and a sprained knee. He is not just physically tough, but mentally tough as well. Within a one-week span, Brett Favre lost his dad, who was his best friend, as well as his brother-in-law to an ATV three-wheeler accident, and yet he still played on *Monday Night Football*, throwing for over 400 yards and four touchdowns. Because Brett Favre is the epitome of *tough*.

Let's examine the personal brand of another public figure whose individual descriptive qualities by themselves may not be as powerful as combining several of them together.

Descriptive Qualities Worksheet	
First Lady Laura Bush	
QUALITY	EVIDENCE
▪ Polished, well-mannered	▪ Dress; how she carries herself and talks with people about the issues
▪ Modest, self-deprecating	▪ Willing to make fun of herself and her husband
▪ Fiercely protective	▪ Passionately defends her husband and watches out for children
▪ Always composed	▪ Didn't lose her cool when insulted by Mrs. Kerry during campaign
▪ Compassionate/gentle	▪ Very high approval ratings; front and center on campaign in '04
▪ Straight shooter	▪ Tells her husband when he is wrong
▪ Great mother	▪ Leads by example; not afraid to scold kids when wrong
▪ Smart/intelligent	▪ Librarian/schoolteacher

When you review First Lady Laura Bush's individual descriptive qualities, none of them may jump out at you the way Brett Favre's did. Some may have come close: *polished, composure, compassion*. But, can she do better?

Are there any other words or phrases she could come up with if she were to combine two or more of her descriptive qualities that would make us feel even more strongly about her? How about:

Benefits Worksheet		
Laura Bush		
QUALITIES		BENEFIT
• Polished, well-mannered • Always composed	}	• Class
• Polished, well-mannered • Always composed • Gentle/soft	}	• A lady
• Modest, self-deprecating • Great mother	}	• Real, authentic
• Straight shooter • Self-deprecating	}	• Honest

If you looked at her initial list of descriptive qualities, you might have been tempted to select one of those qualities as Laura Bush's personal brand. In this phase of the process, we encourage you to push yourself to use your imagination as much as possible. Oftentimes the difference between a good personal brand and a great one is nuance. And those who are willing to labor over the smallest details routinely produce a more compelling personal brand.

Winning an Olympic gold medal makes this point perfectly. What does the winner of the men's Olympic 100-meter race get? That's right, a gold medal. What does that gold medal mean in terms of endorsements and financial gain? Right again—millions!

What does the runner who comes in second place get? You got it— a silver medal. In terms of riches, what does the silver medal get the runner-up? For the most part, bupkis.

And yet the difference between first and second place is often only 0.01 of a second. One-tenth of a second is the difference between fame and virtual anonymity. When selecting our personal brand, we should always do whatever we can to refine it and make it just a little bit better.

The chart to the right shows how I personally worked through this part of the process.

On page 138 I have illustrated how I combined my own descriptive qualities to come up with some benefits that my target audience may find compelling.

There are literally dozens of combinations I could have come up with. The foregoing are merely seven possibilities. There is no trick or magic to this process. A blank *Benefits Worksheet* awaits you on page 139. Again, strike while the iron's hot!

I want you to once again seek out constructive feedback from your peer group. Let them see exactly how you arrived at the benefits you identified for yourself (i.e., which descriptive qualities you combined to produce each specific benefit) and invite them to give you unfiltered feedback. Which benefits do they like best, and why? Encourage them to cross out ones they don't find compelling. Tell them to feel free to put together their own combinations.

Descriptive Qualities Worksheet

Tim O'Brien

QUALITY	EVIDENCE
• Accomplished lawyer	• Admitted to NY, NJ, CA Bars, 13 years experience
• Highly educated	• Georgetown Law, graduated Summa Cum Laude from college
• Very charismatic	• My clients tell me
• Great motivator	• Have built a substantial track record of making people better
• Very caring	• 10 percent of gross income goes to charity
• Innovative	• Created Rainmaker U.
• Great networker	• Know tons of people because of Rainmaker U., great connector, always asked to make introductions
• Tough/incredible perseverance	• Built my business from nothing to over $1M in 3 years
• Exceptional public speaker	• $15K/speech
• Excellent instincts	• Paid a lot of money to give my judgment
• Outstanding people skills	• Huge network
• Extremely informed/knowledge-able about personal branding	• Published author, huge client base
• Strong self-confidence/sense of self	• Not afraid to stand alone on controversial issues
• Highly ethical	• Unbelievably protective of my word and honor
• Very blunt	• I tell people what they need to hear

Benefits Worksheet
Tim O'Brien

QUALITIES		BENEFIT
• Educated • Extremely informed/ knowledgeable about personal branding	}	• Teaching
• Great motivator • Excellent instincts • Personal branding expert	}	• Coaching and Motivation
• Extremely informed/ knowledgeable about personal branding • Excellent instincts • Very blunt	}	• Expertise
• Very charismatic • Exceptional public speaker • Outstanding people skills	}	• Entertainment
• Outstanding people skills • Great networker • Strong self-confidence	}	• Connectedness
• Tough/incredible perseverance • Innovative • Excellent instincts	}	• Inspiration
• Very caring • Highly ethical • Strong self-confidence/ sense of self	}	• Decency

Benefits Worksheet		
	(name)	
QUALITY		BENEFIT
	}	
	}	
	}	
	}	
	}	
	}	

STEP FOUR: PICKING A WINNER

Once you have received constructive feedback about your benefits, it is time to select *the benefit* upon which to build your personal brand. Remember, you can only choose one. Trust your instincts. Select the one that is most relevant to your target audience and resonates with you most. Heed the sage words of President Truman: "Take all the time you need to make a decision. Once you do, do not look back or fold in the face of criticism."

Remember, we can only pick one. In my case, it's either *teaching* or *coaching* or *motivation* or *expertise* or *entertainment* or *connectedness* or *inspiration* or *decency.* I cannot be a *motivating coach* or an *entertaining teacher* or a *winner who is a good person.* Trying to be more than one thing to our target audience will confuse them and dilute the impact of our personal brand's message. Our message must be simple, straightforward and unambiguous.

So which benefit did I choose as my personal brand? *Expertise.* I made this selection for three reasons. First, I wanted to be known for a unique skill or talent because this would give me more cache and, thus, more people would have reason to seek me out. My area of expertise, personal branding, is a very narrow discipline and there are very few dedicated experts in this field. Most who claim to have expertise within the discipline of personal branding are image consultants or are experts within the larger category of corporate branding. I wanted to be recognized as one of the first experts within this niche and then to seek to dominate it. I wanted my name to become synonymous with *personal branding expertise.*

Second, I felt that being an expert would allow me to play up my educational credentials. Specifically, I wanted to leverage the fact that I have a law degree and that I earned it from the prestigious Georgetown School of Law.

Third, I almost chose *passionate,* but ultimately decided against it because of the brand of my industry. Typically, the first thing that pops into people's minds when someone says he is a professional coach is, "Oh, so you're like a motivational speaker." This is not how I want to be perceived. I'd like to think I add much more value than just motivation. I see myself as a strategic advisor on personal branding issues. Though I am passionate, I am leery of using that as my personal brand because I fear it will limit me. I want to be hired for my judgment, not just my enthusiasm. Hence, I think *expertise* is the best choice.

So what's that one keyword upon which you want to build your personal brand?

STEP FIVE: A CATCHY PHRASE

Once you've made your selection, it's on to the final step: turning your benefit into a catchy phrase, if appropriate. I add "if appropriate" because this fifth step does not apply to everyone. Sometimes it's best to simply go with a descriptive quality expressed in a single word. For Nelson Mandela it is *honor,* for Susan B. Anthony it is *brave,* and for Cindy Crawford it is *supermodel.* Trying to dress these descriptive qualities or benefits up with a catchy phrase will only dilute the overall impact of each of these icons' messages.

On the other hand, a catchy phrase is sometimes the final nuance that makes all the difference in the world. Laura Bush is *A Classy Lady.* Tom Hanks is *The Nicest Guy in the World.* Pete Rose was *Charlie Hustle.* Ronald Reagan was *The Great Communicator.*

Does your selection lend itself to being turned into a catchy phrase?

CHAPTER SUMMARY

Key Points

- When selecting our domain, we need to think narrow, narrower and more narrower.

- Our personal descriptive qualities must be positive and relevant to our target audience. We shouldn't waste time with false modesty.

- Our personal descriptive qualities mean nothing to our target audience unless they offer them a specific benefit (e.g., Why do people pay to see Tiger Woods play, Tom Hanks act, Nelson Mandela speak?).

- We can only choose one benefit to promote as our personal brand.

- If appropriate, turn the benefit you select into a catchy phrase (e.g., the personal brand *success* may be restated as: *"Everything she touches turns to gold"*).

TEN

Creating Personal Brand Impact

Good news! Now that you have taken the very powerful step of crystallizing your own personal brand, you have a unique point of differentiation that most of your competitors lack. The next step is to start working on reinforcing our personal brand in the mind of our target audience until we become "top of mind." We do this by building *personal brand equity.*

Personal brand equity is the level of positive, residual emotional feelings others have about us and our personal brand. If others have strong, positive feelings about us, then we have accumulated a lot of personal brand equity. Conversely, if others have a negative opinion or no opinion of us at all, then chances are we have a low level of personal brand equity. We build personal brand equity by practicing consistent behavior over a long period of time that reinforces the word or phrase we want others to think of when they think of us.

It's like buying a home. The day we close on our home, it has little value beyond the purchase price. But over time, as we make improvements to the home and land, the property begins to increase in value. As our property becomes more desirable, the price rises.

The first step to creating personal brand equity is to permanently establish ourselves as a memorable personal brand in the mind of our target audience. Below is the profile of a woman with a white star located toward the back of her head. This star represents achievement of at least a minimum presence in the mind of our target audience. The level of personal brand equity we've amassed at this stage is fairly low because we are just starting to establish ourselves in the mind of our target audience.

VISUAL A

Once we've permanently reserved our space, our next goal is to strategically reinforce our personal brand until that star (i.e., our message) moves from the back of our target audience's mind to the front. Visual B below illustrates the second stage of this process.

The objective at this stage is to establish ourselves in the mind of our target audience until we achieve "top of mind" status. Top of mind status means that whenever anyone within our target audience thinks of the quality for which we want to be known, *we* instantly pop into that person's mind. At this stage, we may not be the only personal brand others think of, but we are definitely someone who immediately comes to mind.

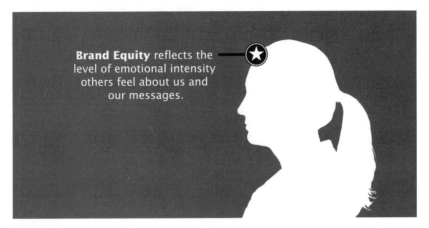

Brand Equity reflects the level of emotional intensity others feel about us and our messages.

VISUAL B

In the third and final stage, our objective is to utilize as many creative strategies as are needed in order to reinforce our personal brand until our star turns red-hot in our target audience's mind and we are unquestionably recognized as the only person our target audience thinks of when they think of the word or phrase for which we want to stand.

We know we have reached this elite status with our target audience when great people within this audience regularly say great things to other great people about us without being prompted by us.

We also know we've achieved red-hot status when we hear comments like, "Oh, so *you're* Bill Clarke. I've heard a lot about you." As you can imagine, this is very flattering, not to mention a significant competitive advantage since we are essentially being pre-sold.

Building this kind of personal brand equity is a lifetime journey. It is not a goal to be attained through a finite number of key strategic gestures. Rather, it is a lifestyle we must commit to live by seven days a week.

Racking up the kind of personal brand equity necessary to build a great personal brand is also very hard work. Quite frankly, that's why there are so few great personal brands. To play on the words of Hall of Fame football coach Vince Lombardi: "Everybody wants to have a great personal brand when it counts, but very few are willing to work at promoting it Monday through Sunday."

I am a case in point. Up until I was 37, I was always looking for the shortcut. I had a girlfriend who once told me, "You start so many things, but never finish anything." Boy, was I steamed, especially because deep down I knew she was right. I was always looking for that one big payday or opportunity for fame. One minute, I was a lawyer. The next, City Councilman. Then an actor. Then a movie producer, and for a period of time back to being a lawyer. As a result, by the time I was 37 I was pretty much nowhere. No career, no wife and kids, no meaningful friendships with people who truly challenged me to be better, and no real prospects for the future.

At the ripe old age of 37, I finally realized that the true road to success is based on hard work. You must pick a course and tenaciously follow it to its end. It's the same thing with personal branding: You must choose a personal brand that is a true reflection of the real you, and then work, day in and day out, to build powerful personal brand equity.

SEEK ADMIRATION, NOT ATTENTION

The mistake most people make when building a personal brand is to shoot for attention. They figure they have hit the mark if they become famous. W. C. Fields once remarked, "Good press, bad press, it doesn't matter as long as you are getting press." I disagree. Attention is not the goal. Glory is. Glory is fame with honor. Becoming famous is not hard. Our goal is to become famous for the right reasons. We want people talking about us out of respect and admiration, not as an object of curiosity or ridicule.

As I write this chapter, the Carl's Jr. soft-porn commercial featuring Paris Hilton, scantily clad, washing a Bentley is in the news. I can't tell you how many people have remarked, "Well, the commercial must be good because we are talking about it."

This shallow analysis misses the point. The goal is not merely to get people talking about Paris Hilton in the commercial. I am fairly certain that Carl's Jr., who spent millions of dollars on the ad, had hoped that the ad would influence more people to buy Carl's Jr. hamburgers. Sorry, Carl's Jr., I just don't see it. As a matter of fact, I wouldn't be surprised to see a backlash from parents who object to this kind of advertising.

Let me give you another example that is currently in the news. I like Tom Cruise as an actor, but he recently made a real spectacle of himself on *Oprah* when he started jumping up and down on Oprah's couch proclaiming his puppy love for 26-year-old Katie Holmes. As was to be expected, there was a small cadre of adoring fans who defended Tom with the tired cliché, "It obviously worked because he's in all the tabloids and they are talking about him on the entertainment news programs night in and night out." The problem is that most of the talk was about how foolish he looked. People who have historically admired Tom Cruise are now laughing at him. There is something disconcerting about a 42-year-old father of two jumping up and down on Oprah's couch on TV screaming, "I'm in love! I'm in love!"[1]

You heard it here first. Tom Cruise's box office appeal will continue to plummet as long as he continues to do and say bizarre things. Like the time he verbally ridiculed Brooke Shields on *The Today Show* for taking anti-depressants. When Matt Lauer challenged Cruise on his expertise on the subject, Cruise became very hostile toward Lauer. Cruise belittled those who have taken medicine. In a matter of minutes, Tom Cruise managed to offend all those who suffer from depression, including millions of mothers who struggle with postpartum depression. My message for Tom is: "People don't like weird, no matter how rich, good looking and famous you are."

---

1. Soon after I wrote this section, Paramount Pictures dropped Tom Cruise as a production partner. The buzz in the industry is that Tom's weirdness has become too much of a liability.

FROM THIS POINT FORWARD . . .

Be on notice. Everything we do and say impacts our personal brand equity bank account: how we dress, how we articulate our message, how we listen, how we follow through, who our friends are and on, and on and on. When I say "everything," I mean *everything*. Every day, we are either adding to or subtracting from our personal brand equity bank account.

What do the following items say about you?

- Your briefcase
- Your business card
- Your handshake
- Your weight, teeth and hair
- Your shoes, tie and belt
- Your car
- Your pitch
- Your table manners
- Your reading habits
- Your immediate friends
- The jokes you tell
- Your language

As much as I want you to take action to enhance your personal brand equity, I also want you to be on guard against missteps that injure your reputation. Be guided by the wisdom of Arthur Ashe: "If one's reputation is a possession, my reputation means most to me. Nothing comes even close to its importance."

There are three guiding principles I suggest you keep in mind when focusing on filling your personal brand equity bank account. Pace yourself. Think small. Exhaust them with your consistency.

IT's A MARATHON, NOT A SPRINT—PACE YOURSELF

Many people become so excited when starting to crystallize their personal brand that they try to fill their personal brand equity bank account all at once. This is an unrealistic goal. Amassing the kind of personal brand equity necessary to build a reputation that precedes you takes a very, very long time. Pace yourself. It takes time to have accumulated the kind of personal brand equity to make things happen. Don't equate slow progress with no progress. Did you know that half of the space shuttle's fuel is spent just lifting off the launch pad? Oftentimes, good things don't pan out for awhile.

Jackie Joyner-Kersee, two-time Olympic heptathlon champion, had a philosophy: Strive to improve just 1 percent in between each competition. I encourage you to think likewise. Build your personal brand equity 1 percent a day.

Let me discuss another episode from my own life that illustrates this point. In 1989, I graduated from Georgetown Law School. I took a job at a mid-tier New Jersey law firm with expectations of setting the world on fire. From my perspective, a mid-tier law firm in New Jersey was lucky to have a Georgetown Law School graduate. Most of my classmates went to larger, often nationally recognized firms. It did not take long for me to get knocked on my keester. Expensive suits, Gucci shoes and all.

The cause of my near-career-ending demise was an error I made when drafting a motion that made one of the partners look bad in front of the court. Not a good move for a new associate with one month under his belt. My personal brand equity bank account was quickly depleted and my overall personal brand appeal shot to the bottom of the barrel. I learned that at one point, the firm was even questioning my hiring altogether.

I remember being completely distraught, going to church every day, praying for direction. All I wanted was to restore my reputation and to do it immediately. The more I pressed for that magic opportunity, the more elusive success seemed to be.

Then one day, during a casual conversation with my next-door neighbor, Dick Mercer, an advertising executive with BBDO at the time, he revealed to me the secret to building personal brand equity. I was sharing with him my troubles and how I was searching for an opportunity to restore my reputation. Patiently Mr. Mercer listened, and when I was done he made one simple recommendation that changed my life. "Timmy [he had known me since I was eleven], just field the ground ball and throw it over to first base over, and over, and over and over again." For some reason this message resonated with me to my core. To this day, whenever I start a new venture, "Field the ground ball . . ." is my guiding philosophy.

The next day, I abandoned my homerun strategy and focused on restoring my reputation one day and one small project at a time. I vowed that I would not move on to another job or law firm until I had fully restored my reputation at my current firm. It took me three long years, but eventually I succeeded. Eventually, I left the firm to pursue other ambitions. When I told the name partner, for whom I was working, that I was leaving, he informed me that he was sorry to see me go because I was one of three young associates whom the partners had handpicked to serve on a liaison committee with the firm's major clients.

It was no different for the greats. Ronald Reagan was known as *The Great Communicator.* I assure you that he spoke to an awful lot of small groups in the middle of Nowheresville long before he earned his now-famous imprimatur. Martha Stewart, like her or not, did not begin as the quintessential hostess on the Food Channel. She catered a lot of parties for a lot of not-so-famous people before she built her mega-personal brand, *Quintessential Hostess.*

Muhammad Ali has a great quote that aptly describes the journey we must follow to build powerful personal brand equity: "The fight is won or lost, behind the lines, in the gym, way out there on the road, long before you ever get to dance under the lights."

DO SWEAT THE SMALL STUFF—THINK SMALL

The second concept to keep in mind when building personal brand equity is: Think small. Harvey Mackay, author of many bestselling books on building relationships, including *Swim with the Sharks Without Being Eaten Alive,* said it best: "Little things don't mean a lot, they mean everything." It's not how large or high-profile the action is, but rather how meaningful.

Thomas Jefferson was chosen by his esteemed colleagues to write the Declaration of Independence. Upon completion of his work, Jefferson asked John Adams to review the document and make any recommendations he felt appropriate. Adams saw fit to make only one single, simple change. Though simple, the change had a profound impact on America's future.

In Jefferson's initial draft, he included the words, "We hold these truths sacred and undeniable." Adams replaced this with "We hold these truths to be self-evident." This small change completely shifted the foundation of the document from, in the words of Ben Franklin, "faith-based to rationale and reason."

Adams' simple change helps illustrate the point that huge impact does not always require huge actions and great drama. Strive, through flawless and consistent delivery of small gestures, to make people feel good about themselves and grateful that you are in their life.

How is it that Mother Teresa, a diminutive, average-looking woman with modest speaking skills, no cell phone, no fax, no office and no fundraising skills whatsoever could capture the attention and respect of the heads of state around the world? The answer lies in the message she communicated to her girls every day before they went out to serve the poor: "Remember, girls, it's not great deeds, but rather little deeds with great love, over, and over, and over again."

NBA great Elton Brand of the Los Angeles Clippers is beloved by his fellow players, fans and especially the staff of the Staples Center.

Why especially the staff? Because he takes the time to remember the names of every single usher in the arena. Oh, by the way, he recently won the NBA's humanitarian award, which essentially means he is recognized as the best human being in the League.

One of my clients, Erik Flexner, recently sent me as part of his "maintaining contact" campaign a small brochure on *How to Protect Your Furniture*. This small gesture had a huge impact on me. The brochure may have been small but its contents were of great value because my wife is a fanatic about taking care of our furniture. She just loved it. What makes the contents of the brochure even more powerful is that Erik's dad is one of America's leading experts on furniture restoration. In a recent meeting with Erik, I praised him for his cleverness and encouraged him to keep it up. "Just a half-dozen more of those small impactful gestures and you will have a buzz about you that others would kill for." His response to me? "That's all well and good, Tim, but how do I come up with them?"

My response: "Figure it out. That's what separates the good from the great. The great are willing to invest the time and mental horsepower that the good are unwilling to do." Erik certainly has the horsepower to do the job. The question is, does he have the willpower?

Another of my clients, Ray Bayat, who is also a dear friend, absolutely blew me away with a gift he gave my wife, Patricia, and me upon the birth of our daughter, Caitlin. The day Caitlin was born, Ray called the hospital and found out all the particulars of her birth: name, length, weight, time of birth, location, etc. He then called a products promotion company and had them wrap a hundred chocolate bars in pink wrappers with a label that read HERESHEIS (i.e., HERE-SHE-IS). On the back label, where the details of the ingredients typically appear, were Caitlin's vital statistics.

The personal brand equity Ray built with me that day was beyond dollars and cents. There is practically nothing I wouldn't do for Ray Bayat and his family.

I was having a conversation not too long ago with a client who had just had a baby. He is a very successful software salesman who routinely posts a seven-figure annual income. I asked him if he was going to send out birth announcements, to which he responded, "No, who am I going to send them to?"

I told him I thought he was making a big mistake. I explained that it is the small, unexpected, classy gestures that separate us from the pack. People expect us to deliver great service, but they don't necessarily expect to receive a first-class birth announcement.

How do I know these little gestures have significant impact? Two reasons. One, I've been the recipient of such gestures and know how impactful they can be. Two, I got chewed out by my childhood best friend's wife, Lauren Mulcahy, because I didn't practice them myself.

When I think of all the classy people I know, the de Cardenas family is always at the top of my list. They never miss a beat. They are the epitome of class. Their Christmas cards, family photos, party invitations, etc., are always top-shelf. It is very apparent that a lot of thought goes into their creation so as to make the right impression.

Every time I receive something from them I always say to my wife, "Hon, look at this. We should do this ourselves." In fact, every year we are so impressed by their Christmas cards that this year I called them to find out who their family's photographer is so that our own Christmas family picture is on the same level as theirs.

This is precisely what personal branding is all about. Being so impressive that others aspire to emulate you.

The second reason I know small gestures have great impact is because Lauren told me so. I did not marry until I was 39 years old. As a result, I would frequently show up to friends' parties solo. These parties ranged from holiday gatherings to baptisms. My eye-opening conversation with Lauren occurred when I showed up to her third child, Katie's, baptism without a gift (for the record, I went to her other two children's baptisms also without a gift).

As I was leaving, Lauren called me aside and gave it to me

straight. "Timmy," she said, "when you show up to a celebration like a baptism you really need to have a gift. You are too old to have bad manners."

Thank God Lauren cared about me enough to set me straight. I was only 27 at the time of our conversation, so hopefully I didn't do too much damage to my personal brand up to that point.

Below is a sampling of small gestures that I have found can have profound impact on our personal brand. Some I do personally; others I have observed colleagues practice:

- Write thank-you notes all the time.
- Call one person a day and tell that person how important he or she is to you.
- Send a small gift to celebrate the birth of a client's, friend's or family member's child.
- Make sure your shoes are shined at all times.
- Express your condolences in person for someone else's loss.
- Never miss acknowledging the birthday of someone important to you.
- Send relevant articles to others that touch them personally.
- Congratulate your adversary on major victories.
- Always make sure your car is immaculate.
- Be the first to contribute to another's charity.
- Say, "I'm sorry."
- Help set up and clean up, especially at functions that might not offer you great rewards.
- Say "Good morning" and "Goodnight" to everyone.
- Take your team to lunch. Invite them to your home for dinner.
- Say "Thank you for your hard work today," to your staff every day.
- Smile a lot.
- Be open, honest and direct with others.
- Give without expecting anything in return.

- Volunteer to go last instead of making sure you are always first in line.
- Have a firm handshake.
- Make the best of tough situations.

We have this tendency as human beings to think that meaningful solutions have to be complicated and difficult if they are to be worth anything. Not true. Remember this mantra: "Simple good, complex bad."

OUTLAST THEM ALL—BE CONSISTENT

Finally, exhaust them with your consistency. Of all the strategies I've employed in my life, my ability to outlast others has been my most effective secret weapon. Combine consistency with the "think small" principle, and watch out.

Here's an example of what I mean. Dress is a powerful and quick way to start building personal brand equity. Expectations create reality. If we look smart, people will give us the benefit of the doubt and think we are smart until we prove them wrong.

My question to you is, does your dress create the expectation that you are:

- Smart?
- Skillful?
- Reliable?
- Trustworthy?
- Disciplined?

We must not just rely upon our own opinion. Ask your peers, family and clients for their feedback.

I personally consider my dress to be a valuable arrow in my quiver. I have one simple rule: I never leave my house unless my wife gives me her seal of approval. "You look like a million bucks" (at least in her eyes). When I say "never," I mean never, including Saturdays and Sundays. On Saturdays and Sundays, I don't necessarily dress in a suit and tie, but I always dress in a style that if I ran into a client or prospect, I would not be embarrassed. I am relentless in my appearance.

Not too long ago, I found myself in my office on President's Day. As always, I was dressed to impress. Upon entering the office, I ran into a friend of mine, Mike O'Callaghan, who is also the name partner in the law firm that occupies the adjoining offices. Mike never passes up a chance to razz me.

"Tim," he teased, "didn't you get the memo? Take a break; it's President's Day. Today's dress is casual."

Without missing a beat, I shot back, "Mike, last time I checked, Shaq doesn't wear his practice uniform to games." Mike and I had a good laugh, but he also knows I was serious.

Did you know that out of respect for the people of America, Ronald Reagan took his jacket off in the Oval Office only twice? Sometimes, President Reagan's staff, who dressed casually on Saturdays and Sundays, would tease, "Mr. President, it's the weekend. No one is around. You can take off your jacket." Reagan would always respond the same, "I don't take my jacket off in the people's office."

Here's one of my favorite stories about dress. I am a member of the Jonathan Club, a private social club in downtown Los Angeles. The maitre d' in the Jonathan Club's Grill Room is an 80-year-old gentleman by the name of Victor Mercado. Victor has worked at the Club for 54 years. Every morning at 7:00 a.m., Victor is dressed in an immaculate tuxedo, ready to greet the members as they arrive at the Grill Room for breakfast. The fact that Victor is never late and is always impeccably dressed is not what impresses me the most. What I admire most about Victor is that every day he rises at 5:00 a.m., showers, shaves and puts on a suit and tie before heading off to work at the Club. Once at the Club, Victor goes into the men's locker room and changes into his tuxedo. At the end of his shift, Victor returns to the locker room and changes back into his suit and tie for the trek home.

Now that's class. Barring none, Victor is the most respected and beloved staff member in the entire Club. He is always requested by the members to work their special events. Victor's brand? *Gentleman.*

Think of what commitment to excellent dress says about a person. It bespeaks discipline, self-respect, focus, class, intelligence, courteousness and good manners.

I must confess, I was not always so committed to the "grooming for success" principle. In my earlier years when I was a know-it-all, I often dressed like a slob and rarely shaved or combed my hair on weekends. Why? Because I could get away with it.

Countless Sunday mornings, my mother and I engaged in the same verbal repartee. "Timmy, aren't you going to comb your hair before you go to church?" I always responded with my customary bluntness, "It is combed. Leave me alone." And out I went. You see, moms understand personal branding long before their children do.

My recommendation to you is to pick six to ten small actions/activities/behaviors that you can consistently execute to strategically accentuate your personal brand. Maybe it is working on your reputation as a person who always shows up on time. My friend, Mickey Siam, recently shared a quote from a friend of his that says it all: "Early is on time, on time is late and late is never acceptable."

It is easy to show up when the events are fun, we're not tired or we don't feel overworked. But can they also count on us to show up when the event is not so hot, the clientele is not our target audience and we're tired? Those are the times when we make the biggest deposits in our personal brand equity bank account—when we do something because it's right and not because we will immediately get something in return.

I once read that President George Bush Sr.'s wife, former First Lady Barbara Bush, encouraged her husband to never miss the opportunity to write a thank-you note. President Bush established the habit of writing four thank-you notes a day. He unfailingly wrote these notes while he was a Congressman, Ambassador to the United Nations, Director of the CIA, Vice President and President.

During the first Gulf War, a journalist asked the president, "How were you able to get so many heads of state from so many different countries on the same page so quickly?"

Bush's response: "I just called my friends to whom I've been writing for years."

I also suggest you write your six to ten items down and keep the list on you at all times as a reminder. If you need accountability, share the list with someone you trust and respect, and ask that person to help you stay focused.

Here's another tip that will help you be more consistent. According to Alcoholics Anonymous, it takes 21 days to plant the seeds of a habit. Practice a specific activity for 21 straight days. Be smart: Choose one activity to focus on at a time, as this will dramatically enhance your chances of success.

CHAPTER SUMMARY

Key Points

- The impact of our personal brand is directly proportional to the level of personal brand equity we amass.
- Everything we do and say either adds to or subtracts from our personal brand equity.
- Building personal brand equity is a marathon, not a sprint. Pace yourself.
- *Do* sweat the small stuff. Think small.
- Exhaust them with your consistency (21-day focus).

Part
THREE

Creating Personal Brand Irresistibility

ELEVEN

How to Get a Jump-Start

If you want to accelerate the process of building personal brand equity, become addicted to: (1) being intentional, (2) hard work and (3) finishing everything you start.

BE INTENTIONAL

Building personal brand equity is all about being intentional. And intentionality is about focus and execution, performing thousands of small gestures over an extended period of time. To further a specific objective or goal, I have just one piece of advice: We must plan our brand equity strategy and then work that strategy as if our life depends on it.

The truth is, however, that most people only flirt with the idea of personal brand greatness. Rather, they subscribe to the mantra of the famous French philosopher René Descartes: "I think, therefore I am," believing that once they choose their brand, the rest automatically takes care of itself. This mindset has no application in the world of personal branding, where only *doers* excel.

One of my clients, John Schafer, recently paid me a very nice

compliment. John is the president of Aslan Realty, an extremely suc-
cessful developer of multi-family housing throughout the western
United States. One of John's partners, whom I had not met, asked
John, "Who is this Tim O'Brien? Why are you meeting with him so
much?" John responded, "Because Tim is the most intentional person
I know."

I don't know if I truly am the *most* intentional person John knows,
but I'll tell you this: I am extraordinarily intentional about being intentional.

As I said in the previous chapter, I didn't figure out that my life's
passion was coaching and teaching until I was 37 years old. And it
wasn't until I was 39 that I zeroed in on the discipline of personal
branding. Coming to the game somewhat late in life, I had a lot of
ground to make up over a short period of time. I knew that ratcheting
up my commitment to intentionality was the only way I was going to
accomplish my goals. This focus has paid off.

Because of our team's intentionality, in just three short years The
Personal Branding Group, Inc., has evolved into a business enterprise
that is easily in the top 1 percent of all income earners in the training
industry. And the exciting part is we think we're only getting started.

One of the simple ways we build brand equity with our target
audience is how we maintain contact with our clients. We do our best
to show them how much we love them. For example, on their birthday, each client receives a card signed by all of our team members. Also
included in the birthday card is a lottery ticket with the following passage: "Thanks for taking a chance on us. P.S. If you win, don't tell us!"

If we want to outperform the competition, we must be more
intentional than they are when it comes to every detail of our business
and personal brand.

Recently, I made a keynote presentation to Lockton Companies, the
largest private property and casualty insurer in the United States. The
presentation was to be made at the Four Seasons Resort in Carlsbad,
California, at 9:00 a.m. one Sunday morning. As is our custom, my team

and I arrived at the hotel 24 hours early in order to ensure that everything we needed to make our presentation a success was in place. For one and a half hours my staff and I combed over every last detail until we were satisfied that everything met our *positively good* standard. When we were done, I thought to myself, I wonder how many other people are committed to this level of preparation? At that moment, the catering staff at the Four Seasons Resort let me know the Four Seasons' answer.

I was standing behind a podium on a two-foot-high stage at the front of the ballroom, facing the tables and chairs where the audience would be seated the next morning. The tables and chairs were set up classroom-style. The point I want to make is so important, I've included an illustration to ensure that you are able to accurately visualize the ballroom's setup.

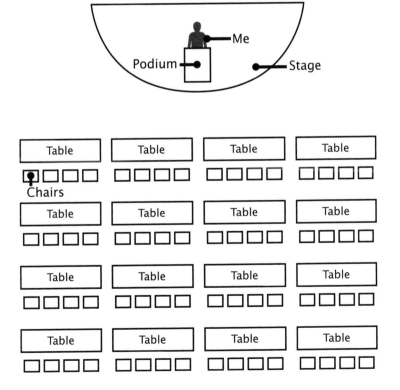

The room was set up to accommodate 150 of Lockton's top producers. At each place setting was a water glass and a pad and pen. What I'm about to describe next is what separates the Four Seasons properties from all others in the hotel industry.

One member of the catering staff's team was positioned in the back of the ballroom holding a piece of string. The other end of the string was being held by a teammate in the front of the ballroom. A third team member was positioned midway between the two workers. These three guys went from row of glasses to row of glasses, using the string as a guide, to make sure all of the glasses were lined up perfectly! If one glass was even slightly out of place, it was moved into perfect alignment. I actually saw the third guy move several glasses just a few centimeters until they were all lined up perfectly. That, my friends, is intentionality!

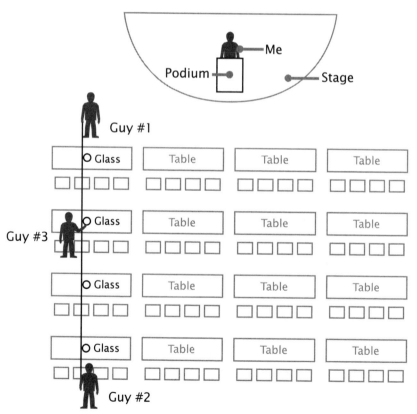

What the Four Seasons knows is that any hotel can buy the best sheets, decorate their rooms so they are plush and hire a first-class chef, but management also knows that very few of its competitors have the kind of commitment to intentionality necessary to create a superior experience. *Experience* is what makes the Four Seasons a cut above all the rest.

The best way to leverage our intentionality is by beginning with the end in mind. Before we take a single action, we must know with total clarity what we want our outcome to be. Then once we have our target in sight, we must go at it with unwavering focus. Random actions, even a lot of them, produce random results. So many people waste valuable time zigzagging toward a goal. What's the shortest distance between two points? You got it: a straight line. Go at building personal brand equity the same way.

For example, before you spend a dime or make any commitments with respect to producing your new brochure, ask yourself, "What do I hope to achieve with this brochure?" Then, make sure each decision you make with respect to that brochure (e.g., color, content, design, etc.) specifically aligns with your overall brand equity plan. Again, lasting brand equity power is built upon an amalgamation of thousands of actions focused toward one single target.

Starting with the end in mind will also result in more efficiency of activity. There is an old sales prospecting adage that I used earlier in the book: "Spray and pray." This means throw enough junk out there, covering as much ground as possible, and something is bound to stick. Don't do this. You'll exhaust yourself.

I have a client, who is also a dear friend, who drives me nuts on occasion with all his zigzagging. He has such potential, but he dilutes the impact of his actions because he operates like one of those automatic sprinkler systems on the golf course, randomly spraying water all over the place. At times, I feel like I'm chasing Ricochet Rabbit around. He has a habit of starting a new, great idea and before he fully implements that idea, he's on to a new one. The result is, he has a lot of great projects going on simultaneously, but not much to speak of in terms of economic payoff.

Through our work together, he's become much more focused. The primary tool we've used to help him is *defined outcomes*. Before we started our work together, he was never really clear about his desired outcomes. Once we were able to help him crystallize the important outcomes he wanted to achieve, Ricochet Rabbit turned into the Rocketman! The improvement has been dramatic.

This client recently paid me a wonderful compliment. He told me that because of what I did for him and his business, in his mind I was a $100,000-a-year coach. The truth is I am no Svengali. All I did was help him focus. This client's talent took care of the rest.

As stated in the previous chapter, my recommendation is to create an exhaustive list of all of the actions you think will help you make deposits into your personal brand equity bank account. Then implement them one by one, not starting on a new strategy until the previous one has been fully completed.

When It Comes to Change, Start with Yourself

It's always best to start with the things we need to change about ourselves *personally*—our habits, communication style and attitude. Once we're squared away as individuals, then we should move on to the supporting props such as our websites, brochures, office space and systems improvements.

A client of mine, Eric Snyder, recently shared with me the key to his success in building a great personal brand. Eric is convinced that building a great personal brand starts with a compelling vision statement. For Eric, everything he does and says has to be in alignment with his personal vision statement, which is: "To be a Trusted Connector Inspiring the Extraordinary."

Most people usually make the mistake of tackling the supporting props first because that's easier and less threatening. After all, who likes to admit they need to change? But I am telling you, if we want to accelerate the accumulation of personal brand equity, we must focus first on changing ourselves. Unfortunately, most people don't have a clue about their own shortcomings.

I recently went to a luncheon called the Treasures of Los Angeles, where the attendees celebrate some of the people of Los Angeles who have had significant, positive impact on the city over an extended period of time. Those celebrated range from real estate developers to police officers, to actors and musicians. On this occasion, I had the displeasure of sitting next to a guy who was one of the most negative people I've ever met. I am not overstating the situation. For 60 minutes, this guy ripped on everyone, including those being honored. I began to grow depressed being around this guy. Finally, I had to excuse myself.

I'll bet a million dollars this guy doesn't have a clue how toxic he is. If you told him he needed to change something about himself personally, I'm sure his response would be, "Who? Me?" All the external changes in the world (e.g., websites, brochures, marketing letters, etc.) will have little or no impact on this guy's success until he makes a fundamental change in his core attitude.

A final comment about intentionality: If you can truly master this discipline, you will be stunned by how fast you blow past the competition. The great poet Henry David Thoreau once said, "Most people live lives of quiet desperation." I think most people's desperation is caused by living their lives randomly. I've found in my experience as a coach that most people's strategy is to do "a little of this and a little of that," reacting to circumstances as opposed to driving results.

One of the most extraordinary tools I've come across for building powerful personal brand equity is the 15-Second Commercial. I can't tell you how many of my clients have made a commitment to me and themselves to script out their own 15-Second Commercial. Probably 5 percent ever follow through. Invariably, something else that is easier to do comes along and captures their attention.

There is absolutely no doubt in my mind that my 15-Second Commercial has produced at least $500,000 in new business for me. If there is one thing I am better at than most of my competition, it is articulating my message in a way that captures people's attention. During Year One, Session B of Rainmaker U., I teach my clients the exact formula I have used. And yet, so few are willing to master this tool.

Our esteemed 28th president, Woodrow Wilson, said it best: "Potential is no match for intentional action."

HARD WORK

The second principle for building powerful personal brand equity is hard work. The best personal brands are the result of hard, in fact sometimes grueling, work. What makes the great personal brands great is that they are willing to do what the average performers are not. There's no two ways about it: Building powerful personal brand equity is a grind. Thomas Edison summed this idea up perfectly: "Most people miss opportunity because it comes dressed in overalls and looks like hard work."

I was reading Lance Armstrong's book *It's Not About the Bike,* in which he describes his training regimen as he was preparing his comeback to the Tour de France after having beaten testicular cancer. It was a cold, rainy, windy day in the mountains of Nice, France. The temperature was in the 30s and Lance was grinding it out on his bike with his coach right there with him . . . driving behind Lance in a car with the heat on! Together they pulled up to a mountain ridge, where Lance stopped to take a break. His coach stepped out of his heated car to survey the road ahead with Lance. After a brief conversation, Lance's coach suggested Lance take the rest of the day off, to which Lance responded, "No way. I must ride when no one else will." Lance went on to train for seven more hours that day. Lance Armstrong would not have earned worldwide recognition and fame as *a winner* had he not been able to dig down deep inside himself and find the strength to outlast them all.

Building the kind of personal brand equity necessary to drive meaningful change can be a lonely job. Many people who meet me today think our success with Rainmaker U. was quick and easy—that one day we decided to create Rainmaker U. and immediately people started joining the program. Nothing could be further from the truth.

It took telling our story to literally thousands of nobodies all over Nowheresville before Rainmaker U. finally caught on. But no matter how frustrated we got, one thing remained constant: Day after day, we made deposits into our personal brand equity bank account so that when our moment did come, we would be ready. I wrote and published articles. Wrote a book. Created and sold products. Changed the way I dressed. Hired a public speaking coach. Changed my daily habits. Improved my manners and etiquette. And on, and on. All *before* we built a successful program.

If you want to be a superstar, you must establish a consistency about building personal brand equity that borders on addiction. I have a client who is so committed to building personal brand equity, it brings tears to my eyes when I think about how far he's come. (Okay, a little dramatic.)

In Session A of our program, we work on something called Standards for Success. These are the rules we commit to live by on a daily basis in order to elevate our game to the next level. Some people refer to them as a Personal Code of Conduct. Standards for Success are so important because they help shape our day-to-day behaviors. They help us stay focused so we become the kind of person people want to know. To help focus our clients in the right direction when crafting their Standards, we ask them, "Assume you are already *The Person to See* with your target audience. What *were* the rules you lived by that enabled you to become that person?" (Notice how I phrase the question so that we get them to begin thinking with the end in mind.)

This particular client actually went out and had T-shirts made with his Standards printed on them, with the writing reversed. Why? So when he got up in the morning to brush his teeth, he could read his Standards in the mirror! The same when he went to bed. He also wore his T-shirts to work under his dress shirts as a constant reminder of how he needed to change.

Finally, hard work requires sacrifice. To me, Mother Teresa is the epitome of sacrifice. A sampling of her sacrifices includes:

- Dressed in old burlap sacks from the store because she and her sisters could use extra money for the poor.
- Rather than spend money on toothpaste, Mother Teresa and her sisters would brush their teeth with ashes.
- One pair of sandals was assigned to three sisters to share. The youngest one was usually given the sandals to wear.
- Wherever Mother Teresa went to banquet, she only drank water so as to not forget those at home in the streets of Calcutta.
- Most of her life, Mother Teresa wore secondhand shoes that were too small. In the later years of her life, her feet grew deformed as a result.

I am not suggesting we aspire to be Mother Teresa to build powerful personal brand equity. Rather, all we have to do is take an honest look at ourselves and pinpoint those self-indulgences, selfish traits or instant-gratification habits that prevent us from making the kind of meaningful sacrifices that will enable us to stand out from the pack. The bigger the sacrifice, the bigger the deposit into our personal brand equity bank account. The bigger the deposit, the more influential our personal brand will be.

FINISHING

Everyone who starts the process of building personal brand equity does so with good intentions. Few finish. Building personal brand equity is not a goal to be achieved. It is a commitment to live a certain way. The process never ends. You've either been blessed or cursed by reading this book. By now you know that having a personal brand is not a choice. The only choice we have is whether we want to define our own personal brand or let others decide it for us. Second, everything we say or do not say, do or do not do, for the rest of our life, either adds to or subtracts from our personal brand.

If you see this information as a welcomed revelation to be acted upon, you are blessed. If you view it as a burden or as pressure, you are cursed. Thomas Edison saw it as a blessing. He was a true finisher. He died at the age of 88 dreaming about his 1,084th patent. (Incidentally, Edison only went as far as the third grade in school.) When most septuagenarians are choosing their gravesite, John Glenn, at the age of 77, was orbiting the earth 134 times. Michelangelo died in the middle of sculpting another Pieta at the age of 84. It did not matter to each of these men that they had solidified their place in history long before their 70s and 80s. They knew only one way to live. Sensing the end, Edison famously lamented, "I would happily give it all up for just more time."

During your journey, you will experience peaks and valleys. Even Winston Churchill, arguably the greatest leader of the 20th century, had long stretches of time when nothing seemed to happen. Even worse, at times, he actually appeared to be going backward.

In 1911, Churchill burst onto the scene as First Lord of the Admiralty, only to have to resign ignominiously following the disaster at Gallipoli. In 1921, he made a comeback only to be run out of office in 1922, branded a warmonger. Much to Churchill's delight, in 1940, with England facing annihilation, placards went up around the country screaming, "Bring Winston back!" Then, after nearly single-handedly leading the West's defeat of Hitler, Churchill was summarily dumped from office. In 1951, he made a brief, ill-advised comeback, which last-ed only four years.

If you study Churchill's life, one thing you will notice about him is that he was the ultimate finisher. He never stopped believing in him-self and, as a result, he never stopped making deposits into his personal brand equity bank account.

Churchill's down times were often his most prolific. He wrote books, published editorials and made countless speeches. Even when he was on the outside looking in, Churchill regularly held lavish din-ner parties with the country's leaders to ensure he kept his fingers on the pulse of what was happening. But even more strategically, Churchill wanted to reinforce the belief that when things turned for the worse, he was unquestionably *The Person to See.*

Had Churchill not worked tirelessly to remain in the hearts and minds of the people of England, he may never have had the chance he longed for—to stare down Hitler and save humanity from Hitler's insidious clutches. If you truly understand the state of affairs in 1939, you know that the world needed Churchill. Had Churchill not con-tinued to labor to build memorable and meaningful personal brand equity while exiled from power, he very well may have faded from the public's eye. How WWII might have turned out is anyone's guess.

It is also worth noting that, when called back into service, Churchill never once uttered, "I told you so." Each and every time he returned to office, his exhortations were always the same: "Let's get to work. There's much to be done."

It's easy to build personal brand equity when we are in a good mood. But the real winners find ways to get it done when nothing seems to be going right. When the odds are stacked against us, we will need tools to sustain a positive attitude. Be assured, it's war out there. Statistics show that the average person has 40,000 thoughts a day. Seventy-five percent of those are negative. A child will laugh 300 times a day. An adult, just 17. Studies have shown that there are 51 diseases that are psychosomatic in origin.

But we are the keeper of what goes into our brain. As Zig Ziglar says, "Your input determines your output." I have found that reading books and listening to audiobooks is the best strategy for keeping my chin up no matter the circumstances.

Did you know that the average college graduate reads a whopping 0.7 books a year? No, that's not a typo. If you read at an average speed and you commit to just 20 minutes per day, at the end of one year you will have read 22 200-page books.

Did you also know that if you read just five books on a single subject, you are recognized as an expert on that subject? How many books have you read in your profession?

A study done by USC School of Business also found that if you drive 15,000 miles or more a year in your car, and you listen to audiobooks consistently, at the end of three years you will have acquired two years of college education. Zig Ziglar calls this "enrolling in Automobile U."

Need some objective, scientific proof of the value of reading books and listening to audiobooks? A clinical study done by Dr. Forrest Tennant at UCLA found that a person's blood makeup can reveal if he or she is a high achiever. The high achievers have the most endorphins and dopamine in their blood. Endorphins act as natural opiates by providing a sense of well-being. Dopamine controls neurotransmission in our brains. Why is all this important? Because the same study also indisputably showed that reading motivational books and listening to motivational audiobooks releases high levels of endorphins and dopamine into our bloodstream.

Just as we must manage our personal brand, we must also manage our attitude. It's not coincidence that people with the best personal brands are also the people with the most positive and optimistic outlooks on life. And, according to historian David Landes, "Optimism always wins."

Landes wrote *The Wealth and Poverty of Nations: Why Some Are So Rich and Some So Poor*. Landes summed up success as follows:

The optimists do not always have because they are always right, but because they are always positive even when they are wrong and that is the way of achievement, correction, improvement and success. Educated eye-open optimism wins.

CHAPTER SUMMARY

Key Points

- *Intentionality* is the greatest force for building personal brand equity.
- Building personal brand equity takes *hard work*. That's why there are so few great personal brands with enduring legacies.
- Be a *finisher*.
  - Finish everything you start.
  - We should be building personal brand equity until the day we die.
  - Others will admire us more for the way we lived than for the assets we accumulated.

TWELVE

Your Track Record

Building personal brand equity requires a first-rate track record. We cannot attempt to position ourselves as *The Person to See* in our industry unless we have *something* to position. That *something* is a proven history of excellence. If you are a trial lawyer, it means having won lots of cases for your clients. If you are a politician, it is a laundry list of good ideas that have helped your constituents and made your community a better place. If you are a corporate CEO, it is a profitable company built upon a healthy corporate culture.

I remember when I was just starting my training company, my father would say to me, "You know, what you need to really put you on the map, son, is a couple of Fortune 500 companies as clients." Like I didn't know that! But he was right. I needed some "names" as part of my roster of clients to give me legitimacy.

This morning I was watching Tim Russert's *Meet the Press* with guests Senator George Allen and Senator Joseph Biden, both candidates for the presidency. Tim Russert, who typically pulls no punches, jumped in feetfirst with a question for both senators: "Gentlemen, is Iraq a disaster, and if so what specifically would you do?" Both senators' responses reminded me why senators very, very rarely ascend to the presidency.[1] Neither senator offered specific, concrete ideas. Instead, there was a lot of blah, blah, blah, blah.

Senators spend a lot of their standing in the well of the Senate making speeches. There is very little individual accountability for senators and even less hands-on governing responsibility. For the most part, senators can only take action as a collective entity. Because of these dynamics, it can prove difficult for a senator to ever build up a proven, clearly identifiable track record of specific decisions and actions that have directly impacted people's lives in a positive way.

In contrast, governors have to actually govern. They must manage budgets, build schools and roads as well as care for their poor and less well-off. Is it any mystery that four of the last five elected presidents— Jimmy Carter, Ronald Reagan, Bill Clinton and George Bush—have been governors?

So how do we build a track record worthy of being positioned? You must follow three rules: First, develop technical competence. Second, be a person of action. And third, remember that building a track record is not an end in itself.

BE A SPECIALIST

When honing your skill set, focus narrowly within your area of expertise. If you are a lawyer, what about your lawyering skills makes you so special? Is it your ability to try cases, negotiate on behalf of your clients or open doors closed to others? Choose one area or skill and become better in it than your competition.

We learned just how powerful specialization can be during the O. J. Simpson trial. The first criminal lawyer Simpson retained was not Johnnie Cochran. Rather, it was Robert Shapiro. Why would Simpson do this when Shapiro was not known for his trial skills? The answer is, because

---

1. The last senator to win the presidency was John F. Kennedy, in 1960.

Shapiro is universally regarded as one of the best plea bargainers in the business. When it was obvious that the case was going to trial, Simpson then replaced Shapiro with a top-flight trial lawyer, Johnnie Cochran.

If you think the Simpson case was a fluke for Shapiro, I encourage you to study the criminal prosecution of Phil Spector, the music producer in Los Angeles who has been charged with murdering Lana Clarkson in the foyer of his mansion. Prior to the indictment, Spector retained Robert Shapiro, ostensibly hoping that Shapiro could negotiate a plea deal prior to an indictment. The cost to Spector for retaining Shapiro? A $1 million nonrefundable retainer fee.

Ultimately, Spector was indicted and the case is set for trial. As Simpson did in his case, Spector replaced Shapiro with another highly accomplished trial lawyer, Bruce Cutler.

For my career, my focus is on personal branding only. I want to be perceived as one of the leading *experts* at helping people create a compelling personal brand that has mass-market appeal. It is my goal to have people say, "If you want to be picked as your next company's CEO, to be elected to higher office or to learn how to best present yourself to your target marketplace, you've got to call Tim O'Brien." I am so committed to this one narrow area of focus that I routinely turn down any opportunity that may potentially dilute my focus in the eyes of my target audience.

Once we choose that narrow focus, we need to work to become excellent at it. Go back to school, read all the relevant books, hire a coach, model the masters. Do whatever it takes to ensure that when it is game time, you have the technical competence to deliver. When it comes to growing and improving our technical competence, we need to be like a vacuum cleaner, sucking up every last morsel of knowledge.

One of my clients recently shared with me a statistic that blew me away. He said that the average parent of a student at Stanford will spend $50,000 a year on that child's education over a four-year period. That's a $200,000 investment in education. That same child will spend a whopping total of $1,200 on his education over the next 10 years. That's $120 per year!

When it comes to my expertise, I am self-taught. Since college and law school I've read hundreds of books, listened to hundreds of hours of audiobooks and attended countless seminars in order to credential myself as an *expert*. I call this period my "third education"—my undergraduate and law degrees being my first and second. And you want to know something? Most of my success in terms of wealth and happiness has come from my third education.

Let me share with you how I approached one of my own technical shortcomings. Until recently, I stunk at back-of-the-room sales (i.e., selling my books and audiobooks from the back of the room following my keynote speeches). I learned just how bad I was after a presentation to Cushman & Wakefield's commercial real estate brokers at their annual convention in Dallas, Texas.

I had the honor of being selected as the conference's kickoff speaker. My presentation was "How to Build a Powerful Personal Brand." Let me tell you, I was on my game. I led a workshop for four hours. The compliments poured in for weeks after.

In contrast, the speaker who followed me was solid, but not great. His topic was not as compelling as mine and he only spoke for 90 minutes. The biggest difference between us, however, was that I sold $600 worth of products, while he sold $40,000! Do you want to be awesome or effective?

The following Monday, I wasted no time. I called this guy and asked him if I could hire him to teach me to do what he did. I made it clear in our conversation that price was not an issue. I knew I had the talent to do what he did—I just didn't know how.

Unfortunately for me, this gentleman doesn't do one-on-one coaching. Undaunted, I kept digging for someone who could teach me the secrets to selling in the back of the room. Eventually I found him. I was able to hire as my coach the number one salesman in the country for one of America's most well-known motivational speakers. I've never looked back. The investment I made in this coach paid for itself 10 times over in just six months.

When it comes to improving my technical competence, I don't fool around. I isolate the discipline I want to improve and then find the best resource available to provide me with the greatest impact in the shortest amount of time.

BE A PERSON OF ACTION

Beware the man who practices arena behavior. "Arena behavior" refers to gladiators in Roman times who refused to fight until their belts were perfectly buckled, their sandals perfectly tied, their hair perfectly combed, their sword perfectly sharpened. Everything had to be absolutely perfect before they would take action. At some point, we have to accept that things are good enough and it's time to just get in there and fight. As Alfred Adler once remarked, "Life happens at the level of events, not words."

Hall of Fame hockey player Wayne Gretzky put it perfectly: "You miss 100 percent of the shots you never take." If we don't get into the game, match or competition, we cannot produce results.

Abraham Lincoln struggled with this very issue as commander-in-chief of the Northern Army during the Civil War. At the beginning of the war, on the advice of his cabinet, Lincoln appointed the most credentialed military man in the country, George McClellan, to head all of the Northern Army's forces. McClellan, a graduate of University of Pennsylvania and the U.S. Military Academy, was regarded as a master strategist. The problem with McClellan was that he was obsessed with preparation.

Lincoln waited eight agonizing months for McClellan to unleash the fury of his armies on the Southern rebels. McClellan, the quintessential arena behavioralist, never moved. His troops always seemed to need just a little bit more training. Lincoln was eventually forced to replace him with Major General Henry W. Halleck.

Contrast McClellan with Ulysses S. Grant. Desperate for a string of devastating battle victories that could end the war, Lincoln appoint-ed Grant commander of the Northern Army. Up until the Civil War, Grant was a washed-out bum known for failing in the lumber business.

Grant's past didn't matter to Lincoln because Grant possessed the one characteristic Lincoln prized: decisiveness. Grant didn't waste one moment on over-preparation. The instant Grant felt his men were good enough, he led them into action.

There's a famous story about Lincoln's response to complaints by Grant's fellow generals about Grant's drunkenness. Apparently, during his tenure as the commander of the Northern Army, Grant was known to imbibe a bit too much. At one point, one of Grant's jealous col-leagues went behind Grant's back and complained to Lincoln about Grant's unseemly habit, to which Lincoln replied, "Tell me what Grant is drinking and I will serve it to the rest of my generals."

If you want to make a name for yourself, be the first into action *and* don't be afraid to take a lot of it even if initially things don't seem to be going your way. You can't do this if you're bogged down in over-preparation and the pursuit of perfection.

I love the quote by Al Ries: "Your reputation will be better if you try many times and succeed only sometimes, than if you fear failure and only try for sure things."

Our strategy should be to determine what level of competence is good enough to start competing. Get to that level and then get going. We can always continue to improve our craft while we are racking up results.

YOUR TRACK RECORD IS
ONLY THE STARTING POINT

Our track record is only the foundation upon which we build our per-sonal brand. It should never be our end goal. The great poet Ralph Waldo Emerson once remarked, "Build a better mouse trap and they will beat a path to your door." This is not true if they don't know about our mouse trap.

As with polishing your technical competence—don't get bogged down in putting all of your energy into building the perfect track record. Build a solid track record and then focus the rest of your resources on marketing that track record in the form of your personal brand.

Clients will often confide in me that they fear they are not ready to market their personal brand at the highest levels because they feel they have not proven themselves enough. More often than not, this is their insecurity talking. I know because I've been there. I remember being so intimidated by prospects who made $1 million a year. Even though I had several million-dollar clients, I always felt I needed a few more of these guys to legitimize me before I was ready to market my personal brand at the highest levels.

Of course, this perspective was utterly foolish because how much someone else makes is irrelevant to how effective we are at our craft. What I should have realized was, once I had racked up a solid string of successes, I had all I needed in terms of a proven track record to compete at the highest levels.

I read in *Reader's Digest* the strategy former First Lady Barbara Bush uses to determine for herself if she is technically competent at something (i.e., whether she is justified in having confidence in her ability to perform a specific activity). Mrs. Bush does it once to see if she can do it. She then does it a second time to make sure it was not a fluke. If Mrs. Bush is successful both times, as far as she is concerned she has the requisite track record to go forward.

Adopt the same strategy when evaluating whether your own track record is strong enough. Yes, it would be nice to have a roster of Fortune 500 clients before you walk into the general counsel's office of Ford Motor Company to pitch your services as a first-rate products liability defense lawyer. But, just because you don't, it doesn't mean you are not ready. Products liability law is the same whether you are doing it for Bill's Soda Shop or General Electric. If you're good, you're good.

Having blue-chip clients certainly makes it easier to sell ourselves, but if we do not have them, all is not lost. After all, even the great Skadden Arps law firm did not open its doors with a laundry list of Fortune 500 clients. I can't know for sure, but I bet the strategy of the lawyers in the firm was to build up a solid track record with a lesser-known clientele and then leverage that track record to create breaks for themselves amongst America's corporate elite.

I'll let you in on a little secret. The first training client I ever had was the California Prison System and I had to *pay them* to let me do my stuff! For three years, I facilitated a program I created called "Living at the Peak," which taught prisoners basic life skills before they were released from prison. I had to underwrite the cost of the entire program: the supplies, workbooks, food, etc.

But what this experience did for me can never be calculated in dollars and cents. For three years, I was able to practice my craft without fear of being fired for incompetence. After all, I did have a captive audience. And when I decided I wanted to pursue a career in the training business, based upon my work in the prisons, I knew I could perform. I didn't need a Fortune 500 company as a client to convince me that I was good.

Now, once I did start building my company, I zealously pursued Fortune 500 companies as clients, but for a different reason. I knew having a Fortune 500 company as my client would make it easier to sell myself up the ladder.

When building your track record, your strategy should be the same. In the beginning, take any client you can get to prove to yourself that you are indeed the real deal. Once you know you're good, just go for it. Good things happen for those who believe in themselves. Great leaders make their moves before they are ready.

Chapter Summary

Key Points

- A solid track record underlies all great personal brands.
- Become a specialist and then promote your specialty until you are blue in the face.
- Brand yourself as a person of action.
- Don't get bogged down in creating the perfect track record.

THIRTEEN

Your Total Personal Brand

The most compelling personal brands are multi-dimensional. Start thinking well-roundedness. The very best personal brands are so much more than the sum of their professions.

In 1962, President John F. Kennedy hosted a dinner for 49 Nobel laureates at the Executive Mansion. It was the largest gathering to be hosted by President Kennedy and the first lady. At one point, the president stood to toast the Nobel laureates. Kennedy spoke many words during his toast, but few were as memorable as his last before sitting down: "Gentlemen, tonight we have assembled in this room some of the most brilliant minds in the world. Never has so much brilliance dined in this room since Thomas Jefferson dined here alone."

If you are familiar with Jefferson's life, you know he was much, much more than a politician. He was also a writer, the founder and president of the University of Virginia, an architect, a painter and a musician. We all should strive to develop a Jeffersonian personal brand.

I have a client, Tom Carlson, who is a spectacular insurance agent. When I say "spectacular," I am not exaggerating. This month alone he made $500,000 in commissions. My struggle with Tom is that his professional excellence is pretty much his total personal brand identity.

With his target audience he is, in effect, little more than a hired gun. If you need to buy insurance, Tom's your man—hands down. But, outside of insurance, the influence of his personal brand is very limited. If people in Tom's community were putting together a list of movers and shakers who could drive change and influence others to get things done, I doubt Tom would be on that list. And it is not because Tom lacks the ability. Rather, he under-markets himself.

And let me tell you, he has a heck of a lot to promote. Tom's a super father of three and a loyal husband. He's also a cancer survivor, very well educated and truly one of the most generous people I know. Yet, because he does not intentionally work to promote all of these different dimensions of his personal brand, he is more or less a one-trick pony.

Tom is not unusual. We have found that most professionals want economic results and they want them now. And promoting the multi-dimensional nature of one's personal brand will most likely not produce immediate economic results. Developing a compelling multi-dimensional personal brand takes long-range strategic thinking and commitment.

In Year One of our Rainmaker U. program, our focus is on teaching our clients how to select the right personal brand for themselves. In Year Two, we work on building personal brand equity. Year Three is all about promoting the multi-dimensional nature of each client's personal brand. For the most part, the people in Rainmaker U. are already very talented and very successful at what they do. They don't come to us just to make more money. They come to learn how to be influential: to mobilize large groups of people for specific purposes. It has been our experience that a person's influence is directly proportional to the overall appeal of his or her personal brand. The more multi-dimensional we are, the more compelling we will be to others.

Let me ask you a question. Be honest. If we were to remove from your personal brand identity what you do for a living, how compelling do you think you'd be to others (i.e., forget you are a commercial real estate broker, a lawyer or accountant)? For many of us, the answer is: "Not very."

Below are some of the categories we should be thinking about when it comes to expanding the multi-dimensional appeal of our personal brand:

- How well read are we (i.e., the number and different types of books we read)?
- How informed are we on current events?
- Political involvement (e.g., Which party? How articulate are we on our party's positions?)
- Our spirituality/religious affiliation
- The hobbies we enjoy (e.g., wine, tennis, golf)
- Interest in sports (conversant on most subjects)
- Our participation in charities (e.g., time/money)
- Our physical fitness
- Our professional accomplishments (i.e., professional track record)
- Our educational achievements (e.g., degrees)
- Awards we've earned (e.g., personally/professionally)
- The diversity of our networks
- Being well traveled
- Developing our articulation (i.e., expression of ideas and breadth of vocabulary)
- Maintaining a positive, proactive attitude
- Developing an engaging personality

We should view our personal brand as the hub of a wheel with each spoke representing a different dimension of who we are. Following I have included a diagram that represents some of the dimensions of my personal brand that I am constantly and intentionally working to develop. Certainly, there is much work to be done in each of these categories.

There are also many more categories I could add to this list—education, family, diversity of network, articulation, hobbies, well read.

The bottom line is that I want to be perceived as more than just a *personal branding expert.* I am always striving to be a well-rounded individual whom others find interesting and compelling. The kind of person other successful people like to have around.

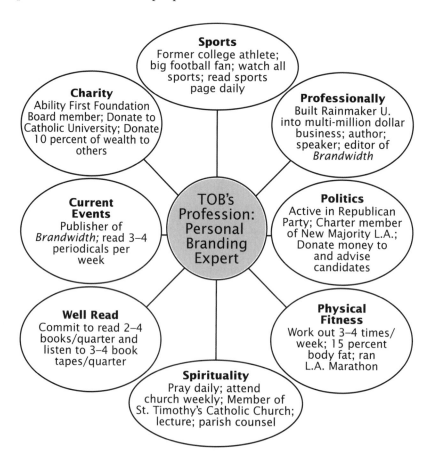

The more interesting we are, the more we will attract other interesting people to us. Think about who we value the most in our society: people with interesting stories. Lance Armstrong. Nelson Mandela. John McCain. What's more, we seek these people out. We want to hear all about what they are doing, and if possible spend as much time as we can in their company. How many times in our lives have we experienced a friend who raced back to us breathlessly in order to share that he just saw or met somebody important?

I remember my friend Scott Duffy recounting how, on the morning of President Ronald Reagan's funeral, he witnessed Mrs. Reagan's motorcade going down Wilshire Boulevard while en route to the memorial service. Because Reagan was such a large figure on the world stage, I was captivated by every detail of Scott's story.

Most of us go through life having to push, push, push to get what we want. Our objective in becoming well-rounded and thus compelling is to create *pull*. We want to be so attractive that other great people pre-sell us to their friends.

Few truly successful people are inspired by the one-dimensional personal brand. We've all been around the guy who has nothing to say unless it relates to himself professionally. I used to work with a guy like this. It was dreadful to spend time with him.

This guy is an awesome trial lawyer, arguably the best in his field. His talent has brought him much recognition and financial gain. It also, unfortunately, has caused him to lose touch with reality. He has become so intoxicated with his success that all he wants to talk about is how great he is. He is also very careful to surround himself with sycophants who applaud his success like otters.

One time I made the mistake of attending a dinner this guy hosted. For three agonizing hours, all he talked about was himself, the law, other lawyers he encountered, his law firm and judges. He never—and I mean *never*—asked any of his guests a single question about our lives.

Well-roundedness is also important because it gives us options. Woe to the professional athlete who spends 10, 15 or 20 years focusing exclusively on his sport. When the crowds disappear, these people often spiral into oblivion because they have not prepared for life after athletics. The smart ones know that life goes on after their playing days are over.

The more well-rounded we are, the more upwardly mobile we will be. Having multiple dimensions is a lot like being a relief pitcher in baseball with many different pitches. If we only have one pitch, we are limited in terms of the variety of situations in which we can be utilized. If we have several pitches, the coach's options to use us are significantly greater. We will also command a much greater salary.

Look beyond your days as a lawyer, doctor or accountant. What else can you do that will make you happy? Perhaps it is heading a non-profit, teaching high school or college or writing a book.

I recently had an idea on which I'm now trying to sell my bride. God willing, my team and I will be able to grow our business to the size where someone else can run it in my absence. Hopefully, by the time I am 50.

If my family is blessed with this financial freedom, I would like to take a one-year sabbatical every five years to pursue a master's degree in a new subject (e.g., psychology, art history, science, etc.). Not so that I can add another degree to my office wall, but to expand my worldview.

I have an undergraduate degree in political science from the Catholic University of America. As an undergraduate, my primary pursuit was not knowledge—it was to obtain excellent grades that would enable me to get into a top law school. This time around, knowledge is *all* I'm interested in. I figure by the time I'm done, I could circle through four or five of these programs.

WOULD THEY PICK YOU?

I want you to imagine you are part of a major charity in your city. Your organization has invited Colin Powell to be the guest of honor at your annual gala dinner. On the dais with the guest of honor are all of the organization's board members, including you. Your board must decide who should sit next to the guest of honor. It must be someone who is interesting, smart, a good conversationalist and well-mannered. In short, the person chosen must reflect well upon the organization. My question to you is: "Would the board choose you?" If the answer is "no" or "I don't know," you have work to do.

I cannot impress upon you enough that one of the goals of building personal brand equity should be to be interesting. Being interesting goes far beyond just having a great résumé. You can be well-rounded without being interesting.

In the 1980s, Pete Dawkins was a candidate for the U.S. Senate from New Jersey. On paper, Dawkins was impossible to beat. A graduate of West Point, Heisman Trophy winner and Rhodes Scholar, Dawkins was about as well-rounded as they come. The problem was, he couldn't relate to people. The rap on Dawkins was he is boring and uninteresting. The consequences of Dawkins' shortcoming were insurmountable. He lacked the ability to excite and mobilize people. He was unable to enroll them in a shared vision. The result was a shellacking in the general election by Frank Lautenberg.

In contrast to Dawkins, Lautenberg was a hustler and entrepreneur who could sell his story well. Lautenberg went on to serve four terms in the Senate before retiring in 2003. Senator Lautenberg was recently called out of retirement to replace then-Senator Robert Torricelli who was forced to resign from his race for reelection ignominiously because of scandal.

Being interesting is hard work. It takes a commitment to ongoing learning, as well as developing the skill of being able to engage others in meaningful conversation. The key to engaging others is mastering the ability to ask the type of open-ended questions that invite others to reveal themselves (i.e., who they are and what they know).

Being adept at engaging others means having something meaningful to share in return. My experience has told me that this is an area where many of today's professionals are lacking. As part of Rainmaker U., we give every class a current events quiz. We will typically ask about ten current events—five cultural and five general-interest questions. A typical question is: "What is the G8 and who are its members?" Rarely does anyone score more than 70 percent. It never ceases to amaze me how so many of us who are so financially successful can be so ill-informed on the important issues of the day. And what's worse, a good majority of us couldn't care less.

Frustrated by this apathy, I have created *Brandwidth,* a non-partisan research service dedicated to informing today's socially conscious leaders on the important issues of the day. Our *Brandwidth* staff selects one issue a month and briefs it from both the liberal and conservative perspectives. Our position papers are fact-based only. There is no hyperbole, opinion or partisanship. All we want to do is arm our readers with the facts on today's most important issues so that when the issues do come up in conversation, our readers are able to weigh in, intelligently.

Some of the issues we have briefed are:

- Supreme Court appointments (judicial activism vs. strict constructionism)
- Abortion
- Same-sex marriage
- Social Security reform
- Pre-war intelligence on WMDs (Did the president lie?)
- The cost and benefits of the Iraq War
- Job outsourcing
- The UN Oil for Food scandal
- Drilling in the Arctic refuge: pros and cons
- Embryonic stem cell research
- New Orleans hurricane disaster (What went wrong?)
- Capital punishment
- The budget deficit
- Immigration
- Global warming

(If you'd like to check out what *Brandwidth* is all about, go to www.brandwidth.info or visit our Products page at www.thepersonal-brandinggroup.com.)

Being interesting doesn't require that we have climbed Mt. Everest without oxygen, backpacked through the Amazon or served in the Special Forces in Iraq. All it takes is exhibiting a basic curiosity about life, people and the world we live in. Just pay more attention to what goes on around you so that you can form and share your informed opinions. The more we know and the more we are able to enrich others' lives, the more people will want to know us.

If we want to penetrate the highest-level networking circles, we need to focus on developing our interesting quotient as much as our bank account. Unfortunately, most amateurs equate their self-worth with their net worth and, therefore, lead with the wealth card.

Superstars will only invite us into their network if we pique their interest—if we can enrich them in a way that they are unable to enrich themselves. Bragging about how much we make or the toys we have will rarely do the trick. In most cases, enrichment means one of two things: providing relevant information or exclusive access.

Remember the movie *Coach Carter?* I have a friend who was able to leverage his friendship with Coach Carter into a relationship with one of the wealthiest, most influential people in Los Angeles. Why? Because my friend knew Coach Carter, and this billionaire did not, but wanted to. Because my buddy was able to get this billionaire access to Coach Carter, this billionaire emails my buddy all the time, inviting him to events that others would give their left arm to attend.

The kicker of this story is how my friend came to know Coach Carter. My friend went to see the movie *Coach Carter* with his fiancée in Westwood, California. He was so inspired by the film that he came out of the theater and got on the phone with his secretary, telling her, "Find out where Coach Carter lives and call him to see if he'll meet with me. If he declines, offer to make a contribution to his favorite charity." Twenty-four hours later, my friend was sitting across the table from *the* Coach Carter. What was supposed to be a polite, one-hour lunch turned into a powerful three-hour bonding session, at the end of which Coach Carter and my friend exchanged phone numbers. My friend had no idea that because of his intentionality in developing a relationship with Coach Carter, he would eventually become email buddies with one of Los Angeles' ultimate power players.

The lesson here is two-fold: (1) We cannot buy our way into the highest circles—we have to be invited—and (2) when the opportunity presents itself, we better have something special to offer.

While most people go through life building their networks randomly, I am very intentional about working to surround myself with interesting people. I want to build the kind of network where people want to know me because of who I know.

Every quarter, I commit to having 40 pull-me-up meetings with stars and rising stars in other industries. When trying to identify people to meet, I focus on finding others who have *skills, resources* or *knowledge* I lack. These meetings do not always translate into new business. I am more interested in "meeting great people who are great at what they do." I do want to meet that person who climbed Mt. Everest, the great trial lawyer who defends indigent inmates on death row, and the principal conductor of the Metropolitan Opera. I want to make sure that, at the end of my life, I don't say, "I wish I had spent more time meeting more interesting people."

Last quarter I was able to set up 36 meetings. I would say that after attending all of these meetings, three have the potential to turn into a real relationship. We won't hit the bull's-eye every meeting. There's no way around it—we have to go through a lot of meetings to find those two or three good prospects with whom we'd like to continue developing a relationship. And when I say prospects, I don't mean just business prospects. These relationships may or may not lead to new business down the road, but that's okay because they will, at a minimum, provide us with valuable life experience.

My wife and I also recently started a new idea to help us gain more exposure to more interesting people. Each quarter, we host the *O'Brien Roundtable Dinner Discussion*. We invite three other couples, so that there are two conservative and two liberal couples. On the invitation we also inform the guests that they are expected to "be prepared to discuss the following issues. . . ." Each new dinner, we invite three new couples and identify three new issues. It is our hope that as we grow personally and professionally, the diversity of the participants, as well as the level of insight we gain through our discussions, will grow significantly.

I've always remembered what my dad once told me was the purpose of life. "Son," he said, "life is about experience. Experience as much of it as you can."

CHAPTER SUMMARY

Key Points

- The most compelling personal brands are multi-dimensional. These people are so much more than just what they do for a living.
- Strive to be interesting. We must work tirelessly on our well-roundedness.
- The more interesting people we surround ourselves with, the more other interesting people will want to know us.

FOURTEEN

The Triangle Offense: Brandits, Brandication, Brandworking

While it would be impossible to give you an exhaustive list of all of the ways to create a great, recognizable personal brand, in this final chapter we will share with you the three major categories of strategies for building personal brand equity. Within each category, there are literally thousands of strategies that can help you make your personal brand great. The objective of this chapter is to give you enough information to get you started.

The three major categories of activities that build powerful personal brand equity are: Brandits, Brandication and Brandworking. What the heck are Brandits, Brandication and Brandworking, you ask? Brandits are the specific habits we must practice in order to reinforce and enhance our personal brand equity. Brandication is the art of using communication to build our personal brand equity. And, as you have by now probably surmised, Brandworking is networking in a way that makes massive deposits into our personal brand equity bank account.

BRANDITS

Building the kind of personal brand equity necessary to position ourselves as *The Person to See* in our industry starts with the type and consistency of the habits we practice. Zig Ziglar, the great motivational speaker, has remarked on more than one occasion, "First make your habits and then your habits will make you."

Habits are the behaviors we practice unconsciously. Human beings are not born with a certain set of habits. Every single one of our habits is learned behavior. Therefore, we are free to keep practicing those that empower us and unlearn those that disempower us.

The first thing we need to do is recognize and stop those habits that are subtracting from our personal brand equity. In other words, before making deposits into our personal brand equity bank account, we must stop making withdrawals.

One of my clients, Tom Gibson, is the president of a very successful technology company. Every day, all day long, while in his office, Tom had the habit of making everyone aware that he was sucking mucus through his nose while at the same time removing phlegm from his throat. To say that Tom's sucking sounds, as well as the visuals those sounds conjured up, were disgusting is an understatement. Unfortunately for Tom, he was the boss, so no one had the guts to tell him just how much he was grossing out his employees. This went on for two years.

Lucky for Tom, he began dating a woman in the company who grew comfortable enough to ask, "Hey, Tom, what's up with the sucking sounds?" Not surprisingly, Tom responded, "What are you talking about?"

This same woman, who eventually became Tom's wife, recommended that he see an ear, nose and throat specialist, which Tom promptly did. Two weeks later, Tom had a long overdue surgical procedure to correct a sinus problem.

The moral of Tom's story is that we often lack the self-perspective necessary to identify habits that are undermining our personal brand. Getting self-perspective is challenging because it necessitates being egoless, vulnerable and honest about our shortcomings. If we can commit to focused self-analysis, even just a little bit, we will find ourselves making leaps and bounds past our competition.

Here's a great analogy that can help us visualize the process of freeing ourselves from our disempowering habits. In the early days of the hot air balloon, the balloon and attached basket were kept from sailing up into the sky by sandbags inside the basket. The balloon would rise only when the captain of the basket tossed sandbags over the sides to the ground below. As he tossed more and more sandbags overboard, the balloon would rise higher and higher. It was only after all of the sandbags had been tossed to the ground below that the balloon rose to its maximum height and glided effortlessly through the clear, blue sky.

The unencumbered balloon sailing across the landscape represents our personal brand equity potential. The sandbags are our bad habits. The great personal brands work tirelessly to toss off their brand-killers, one by one.

I recommend that you gather together a group of peers (1) whom you trust and (2) whose personal brands you admire. For purposes of engaging them in a frank discussion about you, invite them to give you unfiltered feedback about what they see as your brand-killing habits.

The theme of your discussion should be: "Don't worry about hurting my feelings. Let me have it." There are two reasons this dialogue must happen in person. First, your peers will admire your courage and, as a result, will become more emotionally involved in your growth. Second, you've got to convince them of your sincerity so that they feel they truly have your permission to be honest. Most people are conflict-avoidant, unless you can create a very safe environment in which they feel comfortable being totally frank and honest. They've got to see it in your face, eyes and body language, as well as hear it in the tone of your voice.

Here are some of the habits I had to create/eliminate in order to become a more credible player in my industry:

- Admit my mistakes
- Accept responsibility for everything
- Stop putting people down to make myself feel better
- Stop pretending I know things I don't because I'm afraid of looking stupid
- Stop rationalizing my risk-adverse mentality
- Start setting and achieving meaningful goals every day
- Become an early riser
- Stop all antisocial behavior
- Embrace conflict
- Don't be afraid of failing when trying something new
- Always be prepared
- Don't worry about being liked by everyone
- Finish everything I start
- Slow down
- Be more willing to take direction from people smarter than I am

Unless you are a profoundly flawed human being, you will probably find that there are only three or four habits you must change to greatly improve your personal brand. Most, if not all, of the habits identified will also probably be of little value to you. Your discussion with your colleagues should also include the various situations in which these habits manifest themselves so that you can understand what exactly you are doing as well as see the full impact of these behaviors.

I can recall a conversation I was having with a client of mine during which I said to him, "Pete, you are truly a great guy with great potential. You are funny, good looking, smart, an excellent public speaker with great one-on-one people skills, but you have a terrible habit that kills your personal brand."

"What's that?" he asked.

"For some strange reason," I said, "you sometimes say the stupidest things at the most inappropriate time, which causes everybody around you to hate you."

Stunned, Pete looked at me in silence for a few seconds. Finally, he dropped his head and murmured, "I know. I don't know why I do it."

You might think my comments were harsh or even mean. But they were not. I admire Pete very much. He is 100 percent self-made. He is also a great husband and father, and has become a dear friend. I was so blunt with Pete precisely because I care about him. The opposite of love is not hate, it is apathy. The moment I don't care enough about Pete to give him helpful, constructive feedback is the moment our friendship ceases to exist.

The more important point of this story is that I didn't tell Pete something he didn't already know. The only question is, will he change? I honestly don't know. I've been on him about this habit for over a year and he still does the same thing from time to time.

People can change. Just look at George Foreman. When Foreman fought Ali in Zaire in 1974, he was a bad man and proud of it. Foreman came from the mean streets of Houston, Texas. *Mean* was his personal brand. Everything about him was designed to terrorize his opponents.

Several weeks prior to the fight, Ali arrived in Zaire not so much to train and acclimate himself to the grueling heat as much as to mingle with and endear himself to the curious people from this faraway African continent. Ali spent countless hours running through the countryside with the poor children of Zaire, eating lunch with others in open-air cafes in the center of town and doing every media interview he could. By the time of the fight, George Foreman may have been the real champion as sanctioned by boxing's governing bodies, but, more important, Ali was the people's champion.

In sharp contrast to Ali, Foreman arrived after Ali and brashly stepped from the plane's cabin with German Shepherds in tow. What the idiots in Foreman's camp failed to realize was that barking, snarling and rabid German Shepherds were reviled creatures in Zaire because, during WWII, the Belgian soldiers used them to terrorize the people of North Africa. In an instant, because of one misplaced theatrical gesture, Foreman was about as hated as one could be in Zaire.

Ordinarily, the tagline on someone like George Foreman is something like, "And the rest is history." But in Foreman's case his life story was far from over. Not by a long shot.

Fast forward 20 years. Today, Foreman is the darling of the sports, cooking and talk show circuit. Everybody loves George Foreman and nearly everyone who eats hamburgers owns a George Foreman Grill. Why? Because George Foreman decided one day to change his personal brand from *mean* to *nice.*

So how did this metamorphosis occur? The answer is simple. Foreman decided to be *likeable.* Once the decision was made, everything Foreman did and said was likeable. Nothing anyone said or did could get under his skin any longer. Foreman simply made it a habit to be *nice* (instead of *mean*) to everyone. Changing that one single habit changed Foreman's life.

The message to be taken from Foreman's story is, if we pick the right habit(s) to change, the transformation of our personal brand and corresponding personal brand equity can be staggering. The only question to ask yourself is: "Do I have the guts to take on this challenge?"

BRANDICATION: IT'S NOT *WHAT* YOU SAY, IT'S *HOW* YOU SAY IT THAT COUNTS

Once we eliminate our bad habits, it is time to go on the offensive. Communication is perhaps the most powerful tool for building personal brand equity.

Whenever I mention the subject of effective communication, people typically think I am referring solely to public speaking. While unquestionably important, public speaking is only a sliver of the total repertoire of communication skills available to us for building personal brand equity.

In this section I will touch upon just five communication skills:

- Public speaking
- Rapport-building skills
- Asking the right questions
- The art of being a good conversationalist
- Perceptual agility

PUBLIC SPEAKING

Senator John Kerry's public speaking ability was the principal reason he was able to hang on against President Bush in the 2004 presidential race, despite having an anemic personal brand. Because Senator Kerry outshined President Bush so overwhelmingly in the debates, people across America automatically assumed that Senator Kerry is smarter than President Bush, though the facts would appear to tell otherwise.

Both men's academic records are virtually identical. Both attended Yale University (Bush earned his B.A. in history in 1968; Kerry graduated with a B.A. in political science in 1966). Both were C-average students (Bush scored a cumulative 77 percent over four years; Kerry, 76 percent), and both earned postgraduate degrees (Bush, an M.B.A. from Harvard; Kerry, a law degree from Boston College Law School).

But the facts didn't matter because the public's perception was that since Senator Kerry was a much better speaker than President Bush, he must be smarter.

My own situation also illustrates this point. I am no dummy, but a genius I am not. I scored a very modest 970 on my SATs. My LSAT score was just a 32 out of 46, while most of my classmates at Georgetown scored 40 and above. But one skill I have that always allowed me to compensate for any intellectual shortcomings is my public speaking ability. I remember a scenario that occurred during law school that made me realize the power of this skill.

There is a class every Georgetown Law School student has to take called Legal Research and Writing. My class was taught by Professor Johnson. For me, this class was dreadful because it focused on the minutia of legal writing. I would have preferred bamboo shoots being shoved under my fingernails than to take this class. My attitude was reflected in my work. I just wasn't interested in becoming a technically sound legal writer. Unfortunately, Professor Johnson's first impression of me was based upon my written work. And I knew by the way she interacted with me that she didn't think much of me. This all changed when we got to the verbal portion of the class.

As part of the curriculum, each student participated in a mock court exercise where he was expected to argue legal issues before mock judges. The exercise was designed to simulate what it was like to appeal in court. Because the technical aspects of my brief weren't too hot, expectations were understandably low. Lucky for me, when it came time to argue my brief, I hit it out of the park.

My professor was literally slack-jawed when I was done. It was as if she didn't know who I was or where I had come from. In an instant, Professor Johnson's regard for me did a one-eighty.

Now, let me let you in on a little secret. I definitely had the natural talent to do what I did, but when I say "lucky," I mean it. Up to that point, I had never worked to develop my public speaking ability, so the level of my performances in other venues were always erratic and unpredictable. Sometimes I was spot-on and sometimes I was a dud. When I was good, I was great. But when I was bad, I was awful.

The good news is that I finally woke up and realized I had a special gift that I was wasting. I have worked tirelessly ever since to develop my public speaking skills to their fullest potential. I urge you to do the same. Even if it is not your special gift, work at it. People's attention spans are very short. We cannot afford to be boring.

RAPPORT-BUILDING SKILLS

It is true that very few communication skills have the power to catapult you to the front of the pack like being a dynamic public speaker. But for those not skilled in public speaking, do not despair. The ability to quickly develop rapport with another human being in a one-on-one setting is oftentimes just as powerful.

Rapport is the ability to make a connection with another human being in a manner that establishes trust. The talent of rapport-building is an inseparable part of one-on-one communication. John D. Rockefeller once said of interpersonal skills: "I'd pay more for that skill than any other under the sun."

If I had to define rapport in one word, it would be *empathy.* Empathy is the ability to feel what others feel and to let them know it. As the owner of Peet's Coffee once aptly put it: "Without love, it's just coffee." Without empathy, it's just words.

The key ingredient that must be present if we hope to build rapport is the ability to listen. I am not referring to the type of active-listening that sales experts teach us in training classes; I'm talking about listening to people because we are genuinely interested in them. This is about being curious about who the other person is, what he is thinking and feeling and why he thinks and feels the way he does.

Never forget the advice of Mary Kay Ash, the founder of Mary Kay Cosmetics: "Every person has an invisible sign hanging from his neck which says, 'Make me feel important.' Never forget this message when working with people."

Do you ever marvel at the way some people can enter the middle of a conversation and instantly build rapport with all the participants involved? Some do it instinctively, others calculatingly. Either way, their success is a product of one skill: paying attention. They notice things others don't, which enables them to plug in to the conversation at exactly the right time, in exactly the right way. What do these masters notice? Some of their observations include:

- The content of the conversation
- The flow of the conversation
- Where and how everyone is standing
- Body language
- Tone, pitch and tempo of everyone's voice
- Eye contact
- Intensity of everyone's breathing patterns

The master rapport-builders enter conversations on *other* people's level and terms. Once in rapport, they subtly shift the flow of conversation in the direction they want it to go. They are master practitioners of finesse, not force.

ASKING SMART QUESTIONS

If rapport-building does not come naturally to you, all is still not lost. A third Brandication tool that can help us enhance our personal brand equity is the art of asking intelligent, engaging questions. Asking relevant, open-ended questions is a time-tested method for engaging others. Why? Because people love to talk about themselves.

Whenever I find myself in an awkward conversational moment, I instinctively start probing the other person in a non-threatening way about who he is, where he comes from and what his interests are. This technique has yet to fail me.

I can recall an alumni function I was hosting for my alma mater in Los Angeles at the Jonathan Club a couple of years ago. Being the host, I was the first to show up. As luck would have it, the first two guests to arrive were a husband and wife. The wife was pursuing her Ph.D. in Library Science and her husband was working on his Ph.D. in 9th-Century English Literature—two subjects of which I have absolutely zero knowledge. I must admit, for a brief moment, I was panic-stricken. What in God's name would I say to these people?

Running on pure adrenaline, I began asking myself, "What can I ask these folks about themselves?" Out of nowhere popped the question, "So does someone who obtains a Ph.D. in Library Science aspire to be the Librarian of Congress?" My guest smiled shyly and uttered the magic words, "Well, actually . . ." I knew we were on a roll. The rest was easy.

A word of caution about asking questions: Don't ask questions just to ask them. So many people ask questions simply because they either like to hear themselves talk or they are trying to let people know how smart they are.

The people with whom we are trying to build rapport are not dumb. They see these questions for what they are: transparent, awkward and manipulative. They end up putting people ill at ease instead of building rapport.

Whenever I ask someone questions, I only ask about things that interest me. At times the subject of my questions may appear trivial to others. It is not unusual for a listener to burst out laughing at the seemingly frivolousness of my question. I don't care. The key for me is that I am coming from a place of genuine curiosity. The person to whom I'm asking the question always senses my sincerity and graciously responds in kind.

THE ART OF ENGAGING CONVERSATION

The fourth Brandication tool that will help us make bountiful deposits in our personal brand equity bank account is being an engaging conversationalist. Engaging conversation requires the spirited exchange of well-crafted opinions on subjects of mutual interest.

The key to being a great conversationalist is well-roundedness: the ability to talk intelligently about many different subjects beyond the scope of our professional expertise.

I'm here to tell you that the super-wealthy and powerful don't care about how good you are at what you do as much as they care about how fascinating you are. The conversational depth of so many of today's professionals is one-dimensional. All they can talk about with any degree of complexity is what they do for a living. As I said in the previous chapter, take their professions away and you can put their worldliness in a thimble.

I remember my dad saying to me when I was a freshman in high school, "Son, read *Newsweek* or *Time* religiously every week and you will be the smartest kid in your class." I took his advice, and I can tell you that I certainly wasn't even in the top 25 percent in terms of being the smartest, but I do know with equal certainty I could talk intelligently about more subjects than 90 percent of my classmates.

At the same time we are working on our knowledge base, we should also be expanding our vocabulary. Probably not since the days of high school vocabulary tests has the typical professional intentionally added new, more sophisticated words to his vocabulary. Here's a tip: Each new addition of *Reader's Digest* has a section called "Word Power" that is devoted to expanding the reader's vocabulary. As my dad did with *Time* and *Newsweek,* my mom encouraged me to use the *Reader's Digest* "Word Power" to challenge myself to be more articulate. For a period of time, I became so addicted to this idea that I would commit to memory one new word a day. I would write the word I selected for the day on a 3x5 index card and keep it in my shirt pocket the entire day, injecting it into conversations as much as possible.

If we want to take our vocabulary to another level, there are legions of books, audiobooks and seminars available to help us accomplish that task.

THE BENEFITS OF PERCEPTUAL AGILITY

The final Brandication tool isn't so much a tool as it is a discipline. I call it *perceptual agility*. Perceptual agility refers to the skill of being able to see and appreciate all points of view in a discussion, especially when there is conflict.

In every communication exchange, there are three points of view:

our own (first person), the person with whom we are communicating (second person) and a neutral observer who may or may not be present (third person).

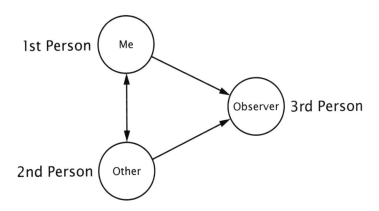

The most effective communicators are able to see and understand all three points of view. Seeing and understanding does not automatically mean agreeing with everyone's perspective. The power of perceptual agility lies in using our understanding of others' points of view for purposes of bridging gaps, overcoming conflict and presenting our own point of view more persuasively.

There is a great story about Gandhi that beautifully illustrates the power of perceptual agility. As the lead negotiator for the people of India at the Round Table Conference, Gandhi would spend hours dressed up in the suits and uniforms of the British representatives, practicing the arguments they were going to make in the coming days. Gandhi would also walk, talk and gesticulate like his counterparts so that he would be fully versed in what the British negotiators would say well before they opened their mouths.

This practice took great discipline, not so much because it was physically or mentally tiring but because it required Gandhi to set aside his ego so that he could, for a brief moment, see and experience the validity of his adversaries' viewpoints. Imagine stepping into Gandhi's shoes and taking on the positions of your oppressors, who, for years, beat you down and considered you less than they. Now that's leadership in action!

Ego is a very common reason most of us fail to practice perceptual agility. We would prefer to be right instead of effective. Winning is more attractive than being accommodating. For some reason, many of us see accommodation as surrender.

Let me warn you about an obstacle you will undoubtedly encounter as you begin to work on your perceptual agility. You are going to come out of your corner, ready to embrace the challenge of experiencing and understanding your counterpart's point of view, expecting him to meet you halfway, only to find that he is firmly ensconced in "first person" and has no intention of budging.

You will more than likely mutter a few choice words under your breath about me and the futility of this process. But if you do, you will have overlooked one critical piece of information. I never said your counterpart would have the same commitment to understanding your point of view as you do to his. It is quite possible that not only won't others be willing to meet you halfway, they won't even come 33 percent, 25 percent or even 10 percent of the way. You may have to go more than 90 percent of the way. Remember the goal: effectiveness, not being right.

How might the world be different if the following great historical figures had remained inflexibly ensconced in their own points of view?

- Martin Luther King
- Mahatma Gandhi
- Nelson Mandela
- Mother Teresa
- Abraham Lincoln
- Winston Churchill

Ronald Reagan kept a wonderful saying on his desk: "There is no limit to what man can achieve if he does not care who gets the credit."

In other words, the people who get the most done are by nature self-less, which is the essence of perceptual agility. If we can surrender our ego, we will be amazed at the horizons that open up to us.

Brandworking: Networking at 30,000 Feet

Mark Twain once said, "You can judge a man by the books he reads and the friends he keeps." We already talked about how knowledge can enhance our personal brand. In this section, I will drive home the point that one of the most common ways people take a measure of who we are is by looking at whom we spend our time with. They want to find out, first, who we know and, second, how who we know can help them get what they want.

If you don't think building a great network is vital, consider that 70 percent of all jobs are found through networking, while 2 percent are found by sending résumés. The Department of Labor predicts that the average college senior will have more than 10 jobs over the course of his career and approximately four career changes. If we don't have a great network, how do we expect to compete in such an economy? Do what Harvey Mackay recommends: "Dig your well before you are thirsty."

The question we have to ask ourselves is, can we and our network help people do things or get things done that they can't accomplish on their own? Can our network solve others' problems? *The Person to See* is the consummate problem-solver.

Let me ask you a blunt question: Do people want to know you because of who you know? They will if you can raise money, get others invited to the right parties, secure tickets to prime events, help others get their kids into the exclusive schools, find a colleague a new job or make critical business introductions. Being able to do any or all of these depends upon the quality of our network.

The Person to See knows everybody. His calls get returned and his requests for favors get answered. People want to do *The Person to See* favors because they want *The Person to See* to do favors for them down the road.

A common reason most of us lack a dynamic network is because we are not intentional about building one. Instead of going out and building the network we want, most of us just let our network happen to us. Our network is usually a random collection of work colleagues, college buddies or friends of friends. Most of our network is also typically based upon social interests as opposed to career advancement. If we are honest with ourselves, we know it is just as easy to be friends with successful, dynamic people as it is to be friends with under-achievers. There is no honor in surrounding ourselves with a bunch of ne'er-do-wells because we think they are "real people."

The best advice I can give you when it comes to building your network is to be intentional. Intentionally identify who you want to meet, why you want to meet them and exactly what you hope to get out of the relationship. Then figure out where these people are, get in front of them and go deep. Be sure you bring value to them before taking.

If we want to build a powerful network, we also have to be willing to log a lot of hours. There is absolutely no way around this. Anybody who says otherwise is lying. Because there is only so much time in the day, we must make our hours count. Being intentional will help us tremendously.

I was recently reading Emanuel Rosen's *The Anatomy of Buzz,* which explains why and how some word-of-mouth messages spread like wildfire while others fizzle out. Rosen states, and I agree, that if you choose the right people to focus on, you'll have all the time you need to go deep.

Rosen's research reveals that the average person can know 500 to 1,500 people at what he calls the *recognition* level, 150 to 500 at the *acquaintance* level and only 11 to 12 people at the *intimate* level. In other words, there is only enough of you to go around with 11 to 12 people.

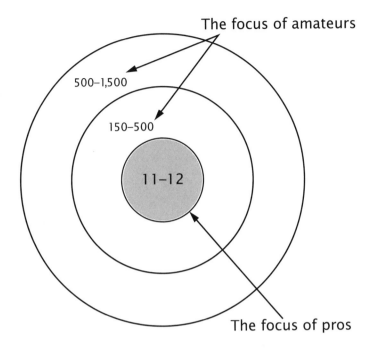

The focus of amateurs

500–1,500

150–500

11–12

The focus of pros

Regrettably, most people spend their time toiling within the *ring of recognition,* or if they are at all intentional they may get within the *ring of acquaintance.*

Stop what you are doing right now and think about your best center of influence. What would it mean to you if you could replicate him just five more times? You probably wouldn't be able to handle all of the opportunity that would come your way. And you'd still have room for those people who could help make your life more interesting.

Right now, I want you to identify the three to five obstacles that prevent you from spending 80 percent of your time out on the street telling people who you are and what makes you special. Are the obstacles:

- Fear of rejection?
- That you don't know who to call?
- That you don't know what to say?

- That you're stuck "in" your business (i.e., doing administrative work)?
- Time management?
- That you don't like it; it feels sleazy?
- That nothing ever happens, so there is no incentive?
- That you have no immediate need to network?
- That you don't have money to do it right?

Figure It Out

Whatever obstacles we face when building our network of superstars, we must overcome them or we will surely be confined to mediocrity. "But how?" is a typical refrain I hear from clients who find themselves stuck. My answer is always the same: "Figure it out."

Most of the time, I know the solutions to my clients' networking challenges, and early in my career I would do the work for them, explaining exactly how to "figure it out." No more. My objective is to teach my clients to be independent, critical thinkers.

I have one client, Richard Charnley, who is currently enjoying a renaissance in his legal career. Richard is an outstanding entertainment attorney in Los Angeles. He is 57 years old and what I love most about him is that he is still hungry to learn. Most professionals at Richard's age figure, "I'm in the sunset of my career so there is not much else for me to learn." Not Richard.

As great as I think Richard is, I must admit that about two years ago his practice hit a plateau. He was representing a lot of insurance companies at an under-appreciated billable hourly rate of $185 to $200—a paltry sum compared to his talent.

One evening, Richard and I were in a coaching session at our regular restaurant on the Westside of Los Angeles. Richard had done everything I had asked of him up to that point in our relationship, except one thing: find and meet more new people face-to-face. It was time for me to have with Richard what I call "a come-to-Jesus talk."

"Richard," I said, "you've done everything I've asked you to do to prepare yourself to go to the next level, except one thing."

"What's that?" he asked.

"Meet more new people," I told him in as direct a manner as possible.

Immediately, Richard became defensive. "What do you want me to do?"

At this point, I could have backed down, but I didn't. "Meet more people," I calmly repeated.

Richard's reaction was to get even more defensive. "You keep saying that!"

"I know," I calmly replied, which I'm sure irritated Richard even more. My attitude was, "Too bad if you don't like it. You didn't hire me to tell you what you want to hear. You hired me to tell you what you need to hear."

"Where do I find these people?" Richard asked confrontationally.

Then I nearly sent him over the edge with my next comment. "I don't know. Figure it out."

You see, Richard had two options: (1) bitch, moan and groan about why nothing was happening or (2) embrace the truth and figure it out. I am happy to report that Richard chose to figure it out.

In literally 12 months, Richard transformed his practice. I kid you not when I say that today Richard works half as much as he used to and makes a lot more money. His billable rate is $450 per hour and he has, through his own efforts, developed a client base that will pay his rate. As we speak, Richard has built himself quite a reputation. He was just wooed away from his current firm by a much larger firm with a prominent national practice.

If we want something bad enough, we will figure it out. Many before me have said the same thing: "If the 'why' is compelling enough, the 'how' is easy." Change happens in an instant. It is the decision to change that takes a long time.

The leverage for Richard was that he could not stand the pain of the status quo any longer. Things had to change. Once Richard fully embraced this mindset, the outcome was never in doubt.

The real winners are hungry for the opportunity to get out there and network, while the pretenders and excuse-makers revel in the minutia of useless activity. Fixing their computer, organizing their desk, preparing the perfect report, and on and on. They would prefer that opportunity pass them by than take the risk that comes along with networking beyond their comfort zone.

My message to you is: "Beware of engaging in treadmill behavior that prevents you from proactively seeking out and taking advantage of opportunities." At the end of the day, everything is our own fault. *Everything*—the good and the bad. Every success and every failure. Blaming, making excuses and complaining won't ever change anything. Only action will.

THE SUPER 100

A second Brandworking strategy we can employ to change the caliber of our network is what I call *The Super 100*. I wish I could claim credit for this wonderfully simple yet powerful idea, but I can't. It was introduced to me by my client Brian Kabateck. Brian is a top-flight plaintiff's attorney in Los Angeles who used this strategy to catapult himself into the Los Angeles *Daily Journal's* list of California's Top 40 Rainmakers.

The Super 100 is simple: Make a list of the top 100 people you know whom you can meet to tell your story. There is one limitation to whom you can put on your list. A person can only get on your list if he or she *can pull you up* in some way. By pulling you up, I mean the person has *skills, resources or knowledge you lack.*

Most amateurs network with only one purpose in mind: "Is this person a prospect?" If the answer is "no," then from the amateur's perspective, the meeting is not worth it. These people are limited because they are thinking tactically. When you create your list, think strategically.

You may find it very difficult to make a list of 100 people. Perhaps you can only come up with 15 or 20. That's okay. The important thing is to get started telling people your story.

As I said in Chapter 13, I commit to having 40 pull-me-up meetings per quarter. I seek out every single one of these people myself. I coordinate the meetings. I pay for everything. Sometimes it's breakfast or lunch, sometimes dinner or an event, or just a cup of coffee.

As I also mentioned, last quarter I was able to arrange only 36 pull-me-up meetings and only three had the potential to amount to a meaningful relationship. Again, amateurs would be discouraged. I, on the other hand, am heartened. I accept that I had to go through 36 meetings to uncover three diamonds. The way I see it, each of these three contacts, by themselves, has the potential to pull me and my business up in some measurable way.

If you have the stick-to-it-iveness to have 20, 30 or 40 pull-me-up meetings a quarter, you will develop a reputation as someone who knows everyone. Not a bad personal brand to have.

A final comment about *The Super 100:* Always strive to play above your head. Look for people who are better than you. I don't mean better as a human being. By "better" I mean people who are further on the path you want to go down.

In 2004, I joined the New Majority, a group of fiscally conservative, socially inclusive Republicans in Los Angeles who work to get like-minded candidates elected to public office. Ninety-five percent of New Majority members are established, financially independent businesspeople. These folks were waaaaay above my head.

What's more, the cost of entry is steep—$10,000 per year. This is ordinary, non-tax-deductible income. I can assure you, I did not have an extra $10K just lying around. The way I saw it, however, I had two choices: (1) make excuses or (2) find a way to make it work. The decision was actually very easy. From my perspective, I could not afford not to join.

I have two principal professional ambitions: (1) Grow my business to the point where I am financially independent and (2) become a strategic advisor on important issues to the President of the United States. The latter goal is not for ego gratification. I love politics and have a strong desire to participate in the decision-making process on today's important societal issues. There was no doubt in my mind that the New Majority would help me with the latter goal, if not both.

Once I decided to join, I was determined to get a return on my investment. I immediately volunteered to help lead the opening of the Los Angeles chapter (the New Majority was actually started in Orange County, California). I also joined the membership committee and was very instrumental in recruiting a lot of candidates in the early stages. Today, the New Majority's Los Angeles Chapter is a vibrant organization and a future force to be reckoned with in local, state and national politics. Because I took a chance and made my move before I was ready, the payoff has been exceptional.

THREE AND OUT

A third Brandworking strategy is *Three and Out*. Every day, I want you to stop what you are doing at 5:00 p.m. and call three people with the specific purpose of telling them that you are in business. I wish I could claim credit for this brilliant idea, too. But I can't. It belongs to another client of mine, Joe Paykin, an attorney in New York City.

For a couple of years after graduating from law school, Joe did what most new attorneys do. They work for someone else. Eventually, Joe realized he was destined to be his own man, so he left the big firm and opened his own practice. There was just one problem: Joe didn't have any clients. Armed with only a phone and ambition, Joe went to work.

Every single day, at 5:00 p.m., without fail, Joe would stop what he was doing and call three people to tell them, "Just wanted to say hi and let you know I'm in business." Over and over again. Slowly, but surely, business began to trickle in. Joe also added every new client to his list of *Three and Out* calls to make. His message to them was: "I really appreciate your business and if there is anyone you think I should get to know, I'd appreciate an introduction very much."

Sometimes Joe reached people live and other times he just left voicemails. The key was consistency. Today, Joe has more business than he can handle—all because he was relentless in spreading the gospel of Joe Paykin.

Call people you've just met. Reconnect with others you've lost touch with. Ask friends to introduce you to others they believe you should meet. Just keep calling without worrying when it will pay off. It's like filling up an empty glass of water one drop at a time. At first, it's as if you are making no progress and then, all of a sudden, that one more drop is all you need to finally see some results.

CONNECT, CONNECT AND CONNECT SOME MORE

If you want to accelerate the process of networking at the highest level, I urge you to adopt an obvious, but routinely overlooked, strategy. Be a connector. Most people pay only lip service to this concept. If truth be told, they are thinking to themselves, "First let me get what I need and then I'll be able to help everyone else." It doesn't work that way.

Zig Ziglar has a great saying: "Help enough people get what they want and you'll have everything you ever want." It's so true. By helping others get what they want, you create an army of loyalists who will want to return the favor.

We make major deposits in our personal brand equity bank account every time we serve as the conduit for two people to meet who would not have otherwise known each other. Of all the brand equity strategies I enjoy practicing the most, connecting is at the top of my list.

By virtue of our program, Rainmaker U., we have developed a large and constantly growing network of successful people. I am fortunate to be the hub of this network. Being the hub enables me to leverage the resources of everyone in this program in a very unique way.

I am truly humbled by the number of requests for help I receive from my colleagues—from helping someone find a job to introducing a client to a graphic designer—all because I have worked intentionally to build a network of superstars.

TAKE THE TIME TO GO NARROW AND DEEP

I recently had a great meeting that confirmed for me that my Brandworking strategy is paying dividends. Shortly after I joined the New Majority, I identified all of my fellow new members who I thought were stars or rising stars. I then set up meetings with them for the purpose of discovering if it made sense to develop further relationships with each of them. I set up six of these pull-me-up meetings. I had no intention of talking business. These folks were so far above me that helping me grow my business would be the farthest thought from their minds. I wanted to meet these players because my instincts told me that I would be a better person for knowing some or all of them.

For each of these meetings I paid the bill. Some were over a meal, others just coffee. Each one lasted at least 90 minutes. I remember one meeting in particular. It was with Don Evans. Don is my age, but we are not in the same league when it comes to success and wealth. Through hard work and business acumen, Don has built up a multi-million-dollar business. He is a force within his industry and a recognizable name in California Republican politics.

Over coffee, Don and I talked about everything except my business. I intentionally focused on learning as much as I could about him by asking a series of probing and open-ended questions. How did you build your business? What are your ambitions? What do you think about this and that issue? I just felt like there was so much to learn from Don, I did not want to miss a kernel of wisdom.

After about two hours, Don finally turned the conversation to me, asking, "Tim, what can I do to help you?"

My response instinctively popped out. "Nothing," I said. And I meant it. "Don, I just wanted to meet you because I thought I could learn from you. I am late to the business game and I want to make up as much time as possible by developing relationships with people like you."

I can't tell you what Don thought. I was coming from a place of genuine honesty, so if he was initially suspicious of my magnanimity, over time he would learn I had no ulterior motives. Eventually, we shook hands, agreed to stay in touch and returned to our respective offices.

As I was driving back, I was thrilled. My meeting with Don, while probably of little importance to him, was a watershed moment for me. I had discovered what it meant to network at the highest level. I would never have permitted myself to squander two to three hours on a meeting during prime prospecting time that did not directly relate in some way to producing business. It was a very liberating feeling not being in a rush. I so enjoyed spending time getting to know someone for the simple reason that he is great at what he does.

Over time, Don and I have become good friends. We've socialized and attended political functions together. Don's friendship gives me so much more than money. It gives me credibility. Rightly or wrongly, people judge us based on the quality of our network. Counting Don as a member of my network is a real personal-brand booster.

Just so you don't confuse my desire to build genuine relationships with people who can pull me up with "status climbing," I'll comment briefly on the other meetings I had with the other five new members identified. Each of the other gentlemen is a player in his own right. Developing a relationship with some or all of them would have definitely added to my credibility the same way Don's friendship has. But it wasn't to be.

I have a very simple philosophy about networking that serves me well. In order for me to go deep with you, I have to like and admire you. If both of these criteria aren't present, a relationship with me will never go anywhere because my heart will never be in it. For one reason or another, these two conditions were not present during my meetings with the other five gentlemen. They may have felt exactly the same way. Who knows? If they did, I am not offended. Sometimes things just don't click. And when they don't—move on.

Today, at least a few of my 40 pull-me-up meetings every quarter are with people who almost certainly can do little or nothing to help me grow my business. And yet, I am eager to meet with them because they are *great people who are great at what they do*. They teach me how to think bigger and become a bold risk-taker.

As much as I want to be financially successful, I also want my life to be interesting and well-rounded. And I have found that the best way for me to do this is to surround myself with interesting people.

Again, people at the top don't care about how much money we have. Ninety-nine percent of the time, they have more than they could ever spend. They are after something more profound. They seek enrichment. Our ticket into the upper echelons is to fulfill these people in a way that they cannot do by themselves. We must strive to make them feel better about themselves because they know us.

CHAPTER SUMMARY

Key Points

- Brandits—We must start with our habits.
  - First, eliminate the ones that result in withdrawals in our personal brand equity bank account.
  - Second, strategically add habits that build personal brand equity.
  - Address one at a time. Remember the power of 21 days!

- Brandication—Look to use communication strategically to make deposits in our personal brand equity bank account.
  - Public speaking
  - Rapport-building
  - Ask smart questions
  - Engaging conversations
  - Perceptual agility

- Brandworking—Mark Twain once said, "You can measure the quality of a man by the books he reads and the company he keeps."
  - The more successful people we know, the more other successful people will want to know us.
  - Work to build 11 to 12 intimate relationships.
  - Make our *Super 100* list, meet with them and tell them our story.
  - *Three and Out.* Make three "Hey, I'm in business" phone calls a day.
  - Be a connector.

CONCLUSION

In writing this book, I have reviewed the many notes I've taken over the years on books I've read, and I came across this inspiring quote:

> *Your improvements should bear some proportion to your advantages. These are the times in which a genius would wish to live. It is not in the still calm of life or in the repose of a pacific station that great characters are formed. The habits of a vigorous mind are formed in contending with great difficulties. Great necessities call out great virtues. When a mind is engaged and animated by scenes that engage the heart, then those qualities that would otherwise lay dormant wake into life and form the character of a hero and a statesman.*

This excerpt is from a letter written by John Adams to his eighteen-year-old son, John Quincy Adams, as the boy was leaving for England to study at Oxford. Adams' words are as true today as they were in the 18th century.

The opportunity before us is enormous. People talk about how the internet has revolutionized the world, but I submit to you that the most profound changes that the internet can cause have yet to occur. Did you know that 75 percent of the world has never even talked on a cell phone—let alone surfed the net? Can you imagine what will happen when the internet really does become universal?

Indeed, change is happening at warp-speed. New frontiers routinely open up to us even before we've had a chance to become fully acclimated to ones just revealed. What role will you and your personal brand play in shaping these new futures? How will you use your influence to make your industry better—to drive positive change? Have the courage to follow the advice of Ralph Waldo Emerson: "Do not go where the path may lead. Go instead where there is no path and leave a trail."

I did not write this book just to teach you how to build a personal brand that will bring you more fame and fortune. At a certain point, a person can only eat so many steaks, drive so many fancy cars, travel to so many exotic destinations. I challenge you to think bigger. Find your own unique greatness so that you can leave your mark on history, as have so many of the great personal brands referenced in this book.

In the words of Henry David Thoreau, "We must overcome the notion that we must be regular. This mindset robs us of our chance to be spectacular." We must not underestimate what we are capable of accomplishing. Each one of us has the capacity to build a personal brand that can make things happen. For some, the impact will be local. Others will be called forward onto the national or world stages by unique circumstances. The key is for each of us to be ready when our personal brand is needed most. Do not underestimate what you are capable of accomplishing.

After all, Charles Lindbergh was a college dropout before becoming the first man to fly nonstop across the Atlantic. Winston Churchill presided over England's biggest military blunder before being called upon by his countrymen to save them from Hitler. General George Patton graduated last in his class at West Point. The first job Justice Sandra Day O'Connor could get after graduating second in her class from Stanford Law School was as a legal secretary.

What made all of these titans of history great was the unbending faith they had in themselves. On May 10, 1940, Churchill had been called back from political exile to serve as prime minister. Records show that Churchill went to bed at 3:00 a.m. thinking, "At last I have the authority to give directions over the whole sea; my past life has been a preparation for this hour—for this triumph. I was certain I knew a good deal about it all, and we are certain to win."

Napoleon Hill would call this conviction "definiteness of purpose." Hill would also tell us, "To have a definiteness of purpose, we have to take control of our minds. We have to believe now what we want to happen in the future."

The future belongs to all of us equally. The only question is, how will we each use our personal brand to make our own mark?

We are eager to hear from you. Please feel free to call or email us, especially with examples of personal branding success stories.

Our contact information is:

The Personal Branding Group, Inc.
515 S. Figueroa Street
Suite 1800
Los Angeles, CA 90071
Phone 213-622-0862
Fax 213-622-0842
www.thepowerofpersonalbranding.com